GET OFF THE BENCH AND BACK IN THE GAME

By

FRANK H. LEAMAN

ISBN: 1-4033-4890-1 (e-book)
ISBN: 1-4033-4891-X (Paperback)

This book is printed on acid free paper.

1stBooks - rev. 12/10/02

Except for the fictional story that opens the chapter, Malnourisment, this book is not a work of fiction. Biblical illustrations are given within the context of their scriptural references. Events and experiences related by the author are true and unexaggerated, but names have been changed.

To my family with love, and in memory of my parents, Eby and Elva Leaman, who taught me about God and supported me with their prayers.

Table of Contents

Forward

This book is intended to inspire the reader to seek a more active and purposeful role in the service of the kingdom of God. It addresses the many problematic events that occur in our lives which we allow to thwart God's intentions for us. Forces that cause us to weaken and withdraw. Vain pursuits and desires that rob us of the opportunity to honor and serve our Creator as we should.

The message of this book is essential for the children of God to heed because of the extreme importance God places on His kingdom. And marvel of marvels, our Heavenly Father desires the blessings of His kingdom for us. He covets our participation. His heart yearns to bless us.

The bench as pictured in this book is a place apart from the activity God has designed for us. It represents inactivity, ineffectiveness, power failure and a famine of blessing. As we rise from the bench to serve our risen Lord, life again becomes meaningful and joyful for us.

It is my earnest prayer that this book will inspire its readers to better recognize the call of God upon their lives and avoid missing opportunities to share in the blessings of kingdom service.

*CONFESS YOUR FAULTS
ONE TO ANOTHER,
AND PRAY ONE
FOR ANOTHER,
THAT YOU MAY BE HEALED.
JAMES 5:16.*

Introduction

At times in our Christian pilgrimage we find ourselves inhibited. Shut down. We withdraw and suffer emotionally, physically and spiritually. The pain can become intense and deprive us of our focus and energy. The causes are numerous. The results are crippling.

This book reviews these causes and offers help for surmounting the difficulties and becoming productive in the work God has planned for us. Consideration is given to the following facts of life:

> That pitfalls in life ensnared our forefathers.
> That life's pathway is strewn with temptation and peril.
> That the price for carelessness and disobedience is great.
> That no one can traverse life's course alone.
> That wisdom, power and strength can be found to avoid failures.

Honesty about our failures and our inability to rise above the tragedies that strike us is essential for our personal growth and wholeness. Raw honesty that expresses how we feel, opens us to receive the support of others. It births through wings of prayer, the encouragement and strength of God.

Honest confession and sharing are invaluable tools for us to exercise to avoid being benched. Life is short. The needs around us are too great to justify time away from the service our Lord has called us to do. The night is coming quickly. And when it arrives, it will cease our labor.

Unless noted otherwise, scripture references used in this book are taken from the New King James Version. God's word has been given to us for our guidance and remains our greatest resource for spiritual growth and happiness.

AND YOU SHALL KNOW THE TRUTH, AND THE TRUTH SHALL MAKE YOU FREE. JOHN 8:32.

Frank H Leaman

Not Being Genuine

Did you ever wonder what the Bible would be like if the failures and sins of God's people were omitted from the writings? What if only the good things people did were mentioned. Heroic acts. Generosity. Accomplishments. Positions of honor. If the Bible heroes could have chosen what was written about them for future generations to read, they would have excluded the accounts of their sinful acts, their willful disobedience and their foolish mistakes. They would have elected to hide the ugly. They would have wanted us to know them as good, righteous, forgiving, fighting for the just cause, holy, loving, purposeful and faithful. Totally devoted to God. Just as we are so tempted to do, they would have chosen to put their best foot forward. To make as good an impression as possible. They would have woven masks of hypocrisy to conceal the reality of their lives.

We would not be able to know them. We could not identify with them. Enshrouded in such falsehood, we would view them as super human. Almost divine. How discouraged we would become! How hopeless we would feel! For within ourselves we would recognize that there is no chance for us to measure up to their perfection. A people who did all the right things all the time.

And we would not be able to know God. How could we understand Him? The depth of His mercy. The magnitude of His love. The totality of His forgiveness. We would not see God disciplining His children in love, picking up the fallen, comforting those in grief, eradicating guilt, healing heart pain. We would not realize that God can redeem us from our plight and save us from our sins. We would consider ourselves beyond His reach as we wallowed in our cesspools of failure. Our despair would crush us.

But God in His infinite wisdom gave us a myriad of snapshots of reality in His Word. He wanted us to be able to see ourselves there. And He wanted us to see Him in action. He wanted to use the Bible to convince us that His love for us is fathomless and His forgiveness is inexhaustible. That none of us needs to live without hope. And He wanted to teach us the value of being real. Of owning our sins and shortcomings. Of confessing our faults one to another so we can rejoice in the miracle of forgiveness.

3

God also gifted us with the perfect example of His Son, Jesus Christ. Dutifully and with steadfast perfection, Jesus followed the purpose designed by His Father. He did not waver from his mission. He gave Himself for us even unto death. To us His commands ring clear. And rightfully so. He purchased us with His own blood. He spoke.

> "Follow me, and I will make you fishers of men." Matthew 4:19.
> "Go therefore, and make disciples of all nations, baptizing them in the name of the Father, and of the Son, and of the Holy Spirit, teaching them to observe all things that I have commanded you." Matthew 28:19, 20.

As the children of God, we want to follow Jesus. There are, however, some questions we need to consider.

> Why do we fail Him so pitifully?
> What forces crush against us and restrict our movement?
> What powers eat away the strength within us?
> What blinds us and binds us?
> What makes our living fruitless?
> Why do we suffer so needlessly?
> Why do we learn too little too late?

Our choices so often are poorly made. We are slow to learn lessons from the failures of others. Many of us have been told stories about Bible characters from our childhood, usually with emphasis on accomplishments rather than failures. Century follows century and records the accounts of those who lived before us.

> Their moments of glory.
> Their times of defeat and disgrace.
> The consequences of their poor choices.
> The destruction and death caused by their sins.

So we are well advised to learn that God wants us to know:

The history of Bible characters, patriarchs, prophets, priests, deliverers, Kings.
The record of Jesus' life and teachings.
The written account of the early Christians.
The history of our fathers.

We also learn from our own experiences. Yet, it is our very nature to blatantly ignore lessons of the past and blindly charge forward in our own strength, following the direction of our desires, relying on what seems right to us, making our ungodly acts to be godly, repeating the sins of our fathers over again.

It is unfortunate that those who were raised in Christian families, privileged with instruction in Bible teaching, were especially sheltered from the knowledge of mistakes, failures and sins that were committed by the Bible characters as well as by their parents, their relatives, their Sunday School teachers, their ministers and others. For the sake of Christian image, family sins and failures are frequently covered with great effort. The effect of this cover-up can be disastrous. Persons can:

Develop a false sense of their own ability to handle the challenges and problems of life.
Become reckless when making decisions.
Be ill-prepared for the power of temptation.
Fail to diligently seek God's guidance.
Stumble and fall like those before them.

In his book *Saints and Snobs*, Marion Jacobson wrote, "We are afraid to tell truths about ourselves for fear of personal rejection and loss of love. We find the task of self-discovery very difficult. We hide truths about ourselves which do not agree with the expectations of the significant people in our world. The assumption is that if these people knew what we were really like, they would reject us and place us outside their circle of love. In a desperate attempt to be loved, we have lost our identity and paraded our masks."

It is in the sharing of our experiences, both good and bad, that we "bear one another's burdens" and together become strong. Birth is given to a sense of community.

5

Keith Miller in his book *A Second Touch*, mentioned that he and his wife prayed with their children at bedtime. There were prayers in which honest confessions of failure as a parent resulted in confession of ill-behavior in the child's prayer that followed. He tells of praying with his five-year-old daughter, "Dear Lord, forgive me for being cross at dinner tonight and help me not to be fussy again. I really don't want to be that way. Please help me to try hard not to be."

To his amazement, his little girl began her prayer by saying, "Dear God, forgive me for teeteeing out in the backyard under the big tree last summer."

When parents own their failures in open confession, their children learn the invaluable lesson that God's love can forgive their wrongdoings and they don't need to hide them. That cleansing is available for the asking. They learn that the goal is to please God and do better the next time.

Who of us is not awed by flocks of migrating geese winging their way across the sky? Our attention is first drawn to them by the sound of their continual honking. As our eyes search upward we spot them. We see them flying in a "V" formation. By flying in this manner, it becomes possible for them to fly seventy-one percent farther than if each bird were flying alone. As each goose flaps its wings, it creates an upward lift for the bird following. Whenever a goose falls out of formation, it instantly feels the drag and resistance of flying alone. It quickly gets back into formation to take advantage of the lifting power provided by the preceding goose in flight. The honking sounds come from the geese flying from behind to encourage those in front to keep up their speed. When the lead goose gets tired, it rotates back into the formation and another goose moves to the point position.

What an object lesson flying geese provide for us! We too can journey through life on the confidence, compassion and thrust we receive from one another. As God's children we join together in formation, sharing a common direction and purpose. The burdens we have are lightened by cooperative effort. How empty our lives become when our ears cannot hear the honking encouragement of others.

There is yet another lesson we can learn by observing geese. When a goose gets sick or wounded and is forced to leave its fellows, two other geese will voluntarily drop out of formation and follow it down to provide assistance, encouragement and protection. When healing and strength returns, they will then rise and fly together, perhaps eventually joining another formation.

There are times when we also become sick and fall. Why should we feel it necessary to hide our failure and wrongdoing, often from those who love us most? The lack of disclosure denies others the opportunity and privilege to voluntarily leave the formation and come to our assistance. And without their understanding, loving and helping, we may never be able to rise from our benches.

Frank H Leaman

*ARE NOT FIVE SPARROWS
SOLD FOR TWO COPPER COINS?
AND NOT ONE OF THEM IS
FORGOTTEN BEFORE GOD.
BUT THE VERY HAIRS
OF YOUR HEAD ARE
ALL NUMBERED.*

*DO NOT FEAR THEREFORE:
YOU ARE OF MORE VALUE
THAN MANY SPARROWS.
LUKE 12: 6, 7.*

Frank H Leaman

Fear

Fear and faith are diametrically opposed. One or the other prevails for every problem we face. How many times our Lord finds us fearful and faithless. It was a fault Jesus frequently charged His disciples with. When we are faithless, our confidence to move forward is shattered and our ability to cope escapes us. Anxiety binds us. Fear paralyzes us. Our circumstances defeat us. We grope for the bench.

We all know the things that make us afraid. The fear of being rejected and abandoned, the fear of making wrong choices, the fear of being truthful, the fear of tragedy and loss, and the fear of illness and pain. Such fears tend to rob us of the peace of trusting in God's provision and protection. It is healing to identify our fears and anxieties and trust in God to renew our confidence and grant us power and courage.

Moses had problems with a people who were fearful. By commandment of the Lord, he sent twelve men into the land of Canaan to spy out the land. Upon their return, only Caleb and Joshua expressed faith that God was able to give them victory in conquest. Caleb pleaded with the people, "Let us go up at once and possess the land, for we are well able to overcome it." Numbers 13:30.

But others said, "We are not able to go up, for they are stronger than we. All the people that we saw are men of great stature." Numbers 13:31,32.

The children of Israel became fearful and angry. They rose up against Moses, Joshua and Caleb, intending to stone them to death and return to Egypt.

Suddenly the glory of the Lord appeared in the tabernacle of the congregation in the sight of all Israel, and those taking part in the insurrection dropped the stones they were holding. Then the Lord spoke, "How long will it be before you believe me for all the signs I have showed among you? Your little ones I will bring in and they shall know the land. You shall wonder in the wilderness for forty years and there you shall die." Numbers 14:35.

The entire congregation of Israel was benched for forty years because the fear in their hearts obstructed their vision of God's enablement. They viewed God as being too small to help them. Their

11

faithlessness bred fear. And fear caused them to challenge God's plan. So God would wait for the next generation to believe in Him.

Fear and worry about our circumstances cause the word of God to become ineffective in us because they smother our faith. We cannot claim God's promises when our minds are filled with anxiety. Worry disarms us. It paralyzes faith.

> We doubt God's love for us.
> We doubt His provisions.
> We doubt His covenant promises.
> We doubt His ability to do what He promised.

Jesus admonished us to take heed that our hearts and minds do not become so overburdened with the cares of this life that we will not be ready for His return. Before we can enjoy the peace Christ came to give us, it is essential that we take our eyes off our circumstances and cast our anxieties on Him. This involves a conscious act of our wills.

There was a time in the life of the disciples when they needed to learn more about faith. Mark 4:35-41. Jesus and His disciples had set out to cross the Sea of Galilee, a distance of eight miles. For Jesus, it had been a day of intense ministry and He was tired. He fell asleep in the stern. It wasn't long before a violent storm came upon them that was totally unanticipated. The Sea of Galilee is about 600 feet below sea level. It is surrounded by high mountains that block the view, so storms can come with little warning. The disciples were seasoned fishermen who were professionals at navigating and managing their boats through storms. But this storm was unlike any they had ever experienced. The wind blew the sea against them with relentless fury and the sea water began to fill their boat. It was as if Satan and his host of demons were attempting to take the life of Jesus. The disciples panicked. They feared for their lives! Finally, as a last resort, they left their stations on the boat and went to find Jesus. He was sleeping through all this, so they hastened to awaken Him. Then they accused Him with the words, "Teacher, don't you care that we are perishing?"

Jesus arose and rebuked the wind and said to the sea, "Peace, be still." And the wind ceased and there was a great calm. This calm happened in an instant. Today, the fishermen along the Sea of Galilee say that after the waves on the sea are stirred up by a bad storm, it takes three days without wind for the sea to become calm again. It takes that long for the kinetic energy of the waves to dissipate. There was something exceedingly authoritative and majestic in this command of Jesus. Standing in the howling tempest on the heaving sea in the darkness of the storm, by His own power, He stilled the waves and caused the wind to cease. It was the power of the Divine to control the phenomenon of the wind and waves that the Divine had created. Then Jesus chided His disciples for being so fearful and for not having faith. The waves of trouble had shut down their faith, even when Jesus was present with them. They could have reasoned that with Jesus with them, they were safe - that the Almighty God would not allow the promised Messiah to perish at sea like this; so somehow, some way, God was going to see them through to safety. But no! They charged Jesus of being guilty of not caring whether they perished or not, saying, "Jesus, you were sleeping. You don't even care about us."

But when the miracle was performed by Jesus, in utter amazement, the disciples questioned among themselves, "What manner of man is this, that even the wind and the sea obey Him?" Slowly, ever so slowly, they were learning that the Son of God was unlimited in His power to help them. The problem in this perilous predicament was where their eyes were focused. Their vision was locked onto the storm and its fury, not on Jesus who had the power to quiet the storm with His voice.

Theirs was a physical storm, but the storms we experience in life come in many forms. Storm situations can cause untold anxiety and they have the power to shut down our faith. Whatever the difficulty, we always have two options. We can worry and conclude that Jesus no longer cares, or we can resist the temptation to fear, and put our trust in the presence of God with us. When we feel panic, that is the time for us to confess our need for God and rely on His love and care for us.

The disciples lived with Jesus, but they underestimated Him. They were slow in seeing His power applied to their situation. And we, like them, often fail to see His power to handle crises in our lives. This matter of faith is a learning process. As the disciples stepped into the boat with Jesus, totally oblivious to the possibility of a storm, they didn't know enough about Jesus. But now, we know the whole story. Therefore, we do not have the same excuse. We know what faith in Jesus can accomplish.

This event shows us that the attacks of Satan against us in whatever form, present difficult ongoing struggles in our lives. Our self-efforts accomplish nothing. Blaming God for our predicaments only accelerates our misery and demonstrates our lack of trust in His love for us and His power to help us. Victory is possible for us in every circumstance, for Christ through His death on the Cross and through the power of His resurrection has made it possible for every one of us to pass even through death victoriously. Therefore, fear need have no power over us. We belong to Christ! He is alive! He is with us! In Him, we have the victory and we cannot be defeated! That is faith learned. That is faith lived.

There was another time when Jesus and His disciples were at sea. Matthew 14:22-32. At the close of the day, Jesus sent the multitudes away and told His disciples to take a boat to the other side of the sea. He remained behind alone to pray. While on the sea, a storm arose and the wind became contrary. Hours passed with the disciples unable to make progress. Finally, during the fourth watch of the night, Jesus began walking across the sea on the water. As He approached the boat, the disciples were struck with fear, thinking that they were seeing a ghost. But Jesus identified Himself and relieved their fears.

Then Peter made a bold request, probably with little thought. "Master," he said. "Command me come to you on the water."

Jesus gave His permission. Peter immediately stepped from the boat and began to walk on the water. Then, he took his eyes off Jesus and looked at the threatening waves. In a moment Peter's faith was stolen by the tempest, and he began to sink. Jesus hastened to his rescue, offering His hand to save Peter.

Had we been there to observe this event, we probably would have yelled, "Bravo, Peter." But Jesus rebuked Peter saying, "O you of little faith, why did you doubt?"

So is the rebuke that comes to us when we focus our eyes on our circumstances rather than on Jesus. Looking in another direction dries up our well of faith. We are often tempted to look behind us. The children of Israel looked back to Egypt when things got difficult for them and lost their opportunity to enter the promised land. Lot's wife looked back toward Sodom and perished. Faith doesn't look back. Faith looks forward and remains focused on Christ, drawing from Him the courage that is needed.

14

God has His purpose in our storms. Storms test our commitment and stretch our faith. Some storms develop slowly and we have time to prepare for them, while other storms burst upon us suddenly and wreck the stability of our lives.

> To look around is to be distressed.
> To look within is to be depressed.
> To look up is to be blessed.

When we fix our minds on the Lord and His purpose for us, we become like the eagle that uses the storm as wind beneath its wings. Then we can rise in majestic power above the storm. We need not allow the storms in our lives to force us to the bench.

Ben Patterson wrote in his book *Waiting; Finding Hope When God Seems Silent*, these words about faith. "The foundation of faith is a firm conviction regarding three things about God - His perfect love, wisdom and power. Like a three-legged stool, no combination of two will do. There must be all three for faith to stand. A strong faith believes that God wills only what is best for us (His love), that He knows what is best for us (His wisdom), and that He is able to do what is best for us (His power).

Many years ago I found a short poem called *The Rainbow's Secret*. I discovered it in an old book of poetry that I purchased at a flea market. It was like finding a treasure. I was struck by the way the poem portrayed despair giving way to hope. At that time, there were some clouds of despair in my life that needed a rainbow of hope. I copied the poem onto an index card modifying some of the lines and committed it to memory. This is how I remember it.

> The sky is dark with sullen clouds;
> The fields are sad with rain;
> When breaks a light beyond the hills
> That shines upon the plain.
>
> And eyes that seldom look above
> Are lifted up on high;
> With hope hearts beat to behold
> A rainbow in the sky.

15

Heaven touches earth on every side
Displayed for all to see;
Wher'er we stand, the rainbow rests,
And we have found a key.

In our times of despair and storm, it helps to realize that eyes that look upward will find God's rainbows.

Storms can become springboards for us. Difficult times beckon us to grow. Reflect for a moment on some eaglets nestled comfortably in the lofty and precarious position of their home. The soft down provided for them from their mother's body has warmed and graced them. They know no hardship. But neither can they fly. So their parent in an act of wisdom and caring intentionally brings adversity. She reaches between her young, pulls the soft down from the floor of the nest and throws it over the edge.

Ouch. Pain. What is happening? Thorns exposed from removal of the blanket of down begin piercing the flesh of the eaglets. In discomfort, they struggle upward. Finally, the strongest reaches the summit and peers over the edge of the nest.

What a glorious moment! The first glance at a whole new world. But how terrifying! Just as the eaglet is preparing to duck back into the nest, its mother places her wing at the nest's edge so the eaglet can walk onto it. Then the mother eagle takes her eaglet for a brief, majestic flight and returns it to the nest. This first step at learning to fly is repeated many times for each of the eaglets in the nest. But the time comes for each one for the next phase of flight training to begin. In flight, the mother eagle tips her wing and the eaglet she was carrying begins to plummet earthward, helplessly tumbling and fluttering. It is unable to save itself from destruction.

But, the eaglet is the object of its mother's eye. Her body is taut, pulled into a swift deep dive. Within moments, she breaks her dive, swoops beneath the eaglet and spreads her wings. She feels the thud as it lands on her back. Then, with majestic powerful strokes of her wings, she carries her young one back to the nest.

More discomfort on the floor of the nest. More struggles to get away from the thorns. More frightening falls from the nest's edge. But there comes a time when weak little wings become stronger and the eaglet learns to soar.

George Muller wrote, "The beginning of anxiety is the end of faith and the beginning of true faith is the end of anxiety. Faith has three stages: little faith, great faith, and perfect faith. Little faith says 'I know God can.' Great faith says 'I know God will.' Perfect faith says 'It is done.'" A faith that has been perfected by surviving the storms we experience is characterized by an unshakable trust. Muller found the prayer of faith to be the key to endless possibilities. He triumphed in establishing orphan homes to care for thousands of English children, trusting God for their daily needs. In his autobiography, he mentioned the following guidelines to help believers build their faith:

1. Carefully read the word of God and meditate upon it. Through reading God's Word and meditating upon it, the believer becomes acquainted with the nature and character of God. Besides God's holiness and justice, he realizes what a kind, loving, gracious, merciful, mighty and faithful Father God is. Therefore, in poverty, affliction, death of loved ones, difficulty in service, or financial need, the believer will rest on the ability of God to help him. He has learned from the Word that God is almighty in power, infinite in wisdom and ready to help and deliver His people.

2. Maintain an upright heart and a good conscience, not knowingly and habitually indulging in things which are contrary to the mind of God. It is not possible to act in faith while grieving the Lord, detracting from His glory and honor. Confidence in God during the hour of trial will vanish because of a guilty conscience and the practice of sin. Faith will be weakened.

3. Do not shrink from opportunities where faith may be tried. With every new trial, faith either increases by trusting God for help or it decreases by not trusting Him. By trusting in God, it is not possible to trust in one's self, others, circumstances or anything else. The more God's child is in a position to be tried in faith, the more he will see God's help and deliverance. Every

17

time help from God is sought and received, faith will be increased.

4. Let God work and don't attempt to work out a deliverance by one's self. When a trial of faith comes, it is natural to distrust God and to trust in one's own resources and abilities. To man, it is difficult to simply look to God and patiently wait for His help. By depending on self rather than casting one's cares on the Lord, more problems are created and faith decreases. Repetition of this practice encourages more self effort when the next trial of faith comes. Stand firm in faith and see the salvation of God. Trust in Him alone. God's timing is always perfect.

We all have times when we question our faith and struggle with fears and anxiety. Facing our fears head-on renews confidence and courage as we realize the power and resources of our loving God. It is not necessary for us to become paralyzed and shut down by fearful circumstances. We can become overcomers in Christ, who has won the victory for us and calls us forward to the field of active participation and joy.

ANGER RESTS IN THE BOSOM OF FOOLS. ECCL. 7:9.

PUT OFF ALL THESE: ANGER, WRATH, MALICE, BLASPHEMY, FILTHY LANGUAGE OUT OF YOUR MOUTH. COL. 3:8.

Frank H Leaman

An Angry Spirit

Anger is an emotion that we frequently misuse. It is a divinely planted emotion that is closely related to our instinct for the right and it is appropriately used for constructive purposes. The Bible tells us of God's anger numerous times. Persons who cannot feel anger at evil, lack conviction for the good. God didn't intend anger to be a weakness in our emotional makeup. He intended it to be a strength. The Bible doesn't condemn anger as a feeling, but it certainly speaks against the wrong quality of anger. It gives warning to those who harbor anger against others because such anger breeds destructive actions.

Constructive anger is void of bitterness, spite, resentment and hate. It works to breed justice and righteousness. It is always controlled and yields it's best fruit when bathed in loving intentions.

An unjustified angry spirit, however, causes us to become uncooperative and unloving. This kind of anger drives us to act in haste, often violently and stubbornly, and culminates in putting us on the bench. While we may rationalize our anger to be just, experience teaches that it seldom is. It creates barriers in relationships and deals out hurt and destruction.

Jonah, a prophet of God, became exceedingly angry with God, so angry he prayed that God would take his life. He had prophesied for years to the children of Israel with little positive results. Then God led him to prophesy to the wicked persons in Nineveh, a city of about one million in number. The entire city from the king to the beggars repented in sackcloth and ashes. Jonah camped outside of the city in a little booth he made for shelter to see what would become of the city. God did not destroy the people of Nineveh. God saw their genuine repentance and stayed his hand of judgment. Nineveh was spared. The heathen were saved from destruction and Jonah realized that God's own people would not be.

Jonah became furious. He told God, "I do well to be angry even unto death." A gourd plant that God had grown for Jonah to shade him from the sun's heat became smitten by a worm. It withered and died. Jonah felt sorry for the gourd plant that perished. Then God underscored His object lesson. He said to Jonah, "You had pity on the gourd. Should I not have pity on the people of Nineveh?" Jonah left his booth realizing that God is gracious, merciful and slow to anger. God never overlooks repentant hearts.

One day, Moses, another servant of God, observed an Egyptian taskmaster beating an Israelite. In an act of anger, he smote the Egyptian and buried him in the sand. The next day, however, he found out that his deed had been witnessed by someone, and word was spreading rapidly throughout the camp. Realizing that it was only a matter of time until the news would reach Egyptian ears, he fled to the land of Midian. There he tended sheep for forty years while his people continued to suffer as slaves in Egypt.

Finally, Moses met God at a bush that was on fire but was not being consumed by the flames. He was informed that the Pharaoh who sought his life had died, and was instructed to go back as God's representative to free the children of Israel from slavery and lead them to the Promised Land. Moses moved from the bench in response to God's call.

Later, there was another time when Moses was under extreme stress and acted in anger. The congregation of Israel was wandering through the desert of Zin. They had no water. Soon a multitude of people gathered themselves against Moses, charging that he had led them into the wilderness to die. Moses entreated the Lord for water.

The Lord said to him, "Speak to the rock before their eyes and it will give forth water for the congregation and their beasts."

Instead, Moses yelled, "Hear now you rebels, must water be fetched from this rock for you?" Then he smote the rock twice with his rod in anger. It was not God's way.

God told Moses that because of his angry demonstration before the children of Israel, he would die before entering the Promised Land. Within several months, Moses was instructed to prepare for his death and to appoint Joshua as leader in his place. His eyes viewed the Promised Land from the mountain top, but his feet never trod its soil. He never tasted its honey.

My mother was raised in Kinzer, a small town in Lancaster County amid the farm country where the Amish settled in Pennsylvania. Her father owned a country store where he sold groceries and basic necessity items. Cooked meals were also provided for men who were enlarging the Route 30 highway. Being the oldest child in her family, she helped her parents by working in the store and cooking and serving tables.

Although her family was faithful in church attendance and her mother was a very dedicated Christian, her father was not committed to the Christian life. At times he could be jolly and cordial, but he was also known to have a very violent temper.

While my mother was attending Eastern Mennonite College, she received a call from God to go to Africa. At the time she was engaged to the man who would become my father. He had finished college and was teaching in a one room Amish school house. Soon after marriage, they became candidates for missionary service for the Mennonite Board of Missions and Charities.

As my parents left for Africa, my mother still had not seen a change in her father in regard to spiritual matters. Although he attended church regularly, his spiritual life was at a low ebb. She wasn't certain if he even was a Christian and made this a continual prayer concern.

One night while sleeping in our little home on the mission compound in Tanganyika Territory, British East Africa, my mother had a dream that troubled her. In her dream, she was standing with her younger sister and brother and her parents behind the counter in the country store in Kinzer. Suddenly a violent wind blew the roof away from the building. The store became filled with a brilliant light. Looking upward, she saw Jesus in indescribable glory, His long white garments flowed in the breeze. His eyes sparkled like diamonds. His hair was white like wool. His face was the expression of joy. He extended His arms in a beckoning gesture for them to come and join Him in the air.

My mother's heart pounded furiously. As she watched, she saw her younger sister begin to ascend to be with Jesus. Then her brother began to ascend to meet Jesus. Next, her mother began to ascend in exclamations of praise and joy. Then she began ascend.

But looking back, she saw a terribly hopeless look in her father's eyes. "Daddy come with us," she shouted.

Painfully, with deep lines of horror across his face, he cried, "I can't come with you. I'm not ready. I can't come along."

In another moment she awoke in anxiety and sweat. She wakened my father and told him about the her dream. They sensed that my grandfather was in grave danger. They knelt on the concrete floor beside their bed and cried out to the Lord to spare his life and save his soul. After heart rending prayer, the Lord gave them assurance and peace.

At the time of my mother's dream, unknown to her, my grandfather was being rushed to the hospital. He had been involved in a serious automobile accident that caused a critical concussional injury. God answered prayer. His life was spared.

Through that experience, he yielded his life completely to the Lord. His temper became controlled by Jesus, his new Master. Finally, after many years, he was able to move from the bench and witness about the victory that the Lord gave him. You could not meet a happier man. People who knew him were surprised at the change in him.

The injury he sustained, however, formed a tumor against his brain. At times it caused him excruciating pain that wouldn't allow him to function. Doctors and specialists could do nothing to help him. The tumor was determined to be inoperable. He suffered greatly for a number of years. During this time, he attended several healing services and went forward for prayer. Although healing didn't come at those times, he developed an assurance that some day the Lord was going to heal him and he told this to his relatives and friends.

Then, while he was running a floor polisher at the Hamilton Watch factory in Lancaster, Pennsylvania, during the night he heard the Lord tell him, "Ike, I'm going to heal you tonight." It was like hearing God's voice distinctly within his mind. Not an audible voice.

He left the polisher and went into the men's lounge to pray. The entire room became enveloped in thick darkness. He could feel an intense evil presence all about him that seemed to block his praying. Soon he was drenched in perspiration. He did not have a headache at that time and sensed that he hadn't been healed, but felt pressured to return to the floor polisher to get his work done.

Again, while running the polisher, he heard God's voice repeating the exact words he had heard before. Another trip to the men's lounge. Another battle with the demonic darkness. After no apparent breakthrough, he returned dripping in sweat to the polisher to continue his work.

Another time during the night this entire cycle was repeated with no apparent breakthrough. No sense of victory. No assurance of healing.

Finally, at six o'clock in the morning he put the polisher away, went into the men's lounge and locked the door. In earnest he began praying, "Lord, the night is about over and you promised to heal me tonight. Workers will be arriving here in thirty minutes. The time for my healing must be now."

In an instant the darkness that had closed in about him was banished. A glorious brilliant light flooded the room. His very soul seemed lifted within him. Although he was experiencing no headache at that moment, he knew that he had been healed. He leaped to his feet praising God. All the way home, he filled his car with songs of praise and exclamations of thanksgiving.

He rushed upstairs and told my grandmother, "The most wonderful thing happened to me last night at work. I know the Lord healed me." His face was beaming. He was praising the Lord. Indeed, he had been healed. He never experienced the painful spells again. The tumor that could not be removed surgically without killing him was gone. What a testimony of what our Lord can do!

I can still remember vividly the last evening I spent in my grandfather's presence. It was a Monday evening. The following morning I had to leave home for my sophomore year of college. During that day, my grandfather called my mother and said, "Bring your family over for dinner tonight. I have a cake I baked for company on Sunday and the company didn't come. And have Jim and Betty bring their guitar and accordion so we can sing some songs after dinner."

She accepted the invitation for us. This was the only time my brother and sister took their musical instruments to play and sing with my grandparents.

My grandfather was a tremendous cook. While he was preparing the meal, he took my mother aside and showed her some nitroglycerin tablets that he was taking. He told her, "Your mother doesn't know it yet, but I've been to the hospital. I've been having a lot of trouble with my heart. The doctor told me that I have several traveling blood clots and when one passes over the heart it could mean sudden death for me. I sense I don't have much longer to live. God will be calling me home soon." He explained that he planned to tell my grandmother about his condition that evening while they were together with family.

We all crowded into the living room. My grandfather led us in singing a list of songs that seemed unending. We had a wonderful

25

time together. Before we realized, it was eleven o'clock and we left for home. Later, we recalled that almost every song mentioned something about heaven. I had never seen my grandfather so happy.

At seven o'clock the following evening, my mother received a call to come without delay to St. Joseph's Hospital in Lancaster. She told my father, "My Daddy passed on to be with Jesus."

He replied, "You've got to think more positively. I'm sure if he was dead they would have told us that. He's in the hospital. He's in good hands."

But my grandfather was dead. He and grandmother had picked up two elderly women and were on their way to church for a Bible Study. When they pulled into the parking lot, my grandfather did an unusually poor job of parking the car. He got out and started to go around the front of the car to help my grandmother, when he collapsed over the hood. When grandmother reached him, he told her, "I'm going home." He did.

What a privilege it was to have a grandfather who left me with fond memories. I remember him not as a violent man, but as a saint who was filled with joy and had a beaming testimony of God's goodness. He knew where he was going. By God's grace I will meet him again, not in an earthly tabernacle, but in a glorious body designed for heavenly living. Yes. Praise be to our God. We will sing together again. How glad I am that my grandfather was transformed by God's grace and moved from the bench where an uncontrolled temper had bound him for many unfruitful years.

*WOE TO YOU SCRIBES
AND PHARISEES,
HYPOCRITES!
FOR YOU SHUT UP
THE KINGDOM OF HEAVEN
AGAINST MEN.
YOU DON'T GO IN
YOURSELVES,
AND YOU DON'T LET
OTHERS ENTER.
MATT. 23:13.*

Frank H Leaman

Self-Righteousness and Hypocrisy

While self-righteousness and hypocrisy seldom remove us from the limelight of the stage or the action of the playing field, these traits place us on a bench of ineffectiveness. Our self-righteous rules stifle the freedom of others unnecessarily and rob them of motivation, power and opportunity. Tremendous energy is wasted in forcing persons into molds of our liking. By acting in this manner, we fight against the very purpose of God. Christ came to set men free. Why should we attempt to bind?

When we reflect on these characteristics, our minds rather naturally go back two thousand years in time to the religious rulers in Jerusalem. The Pharisees were very showy in their profession of faith to God. They were educated in the Law of Moses. They had authority. But…

Where was the love?
Where was the compassion?
Where was the ability to recognize Jesus as the Son of God?

Alas, Jesus didn't fit their mold! It's little wonder that they met the teachings of Jesus with such strong resistance. Jesus spoke the truth. The truth was too painful for them to receive. Confrontation was swift in its coming. Jesus denounced woe upon them saying, "Ye fools and blind." "For a pretense you make long prayer." "You pay tithe and have omitted the weightier matters of the law, judgment, mercy and faith." "You strain at a gnat and swallow a camel." "You cleanse the outside of the cup and dish, but inside you are full of extortion and excess." "You appear beautiful outwardly, but inside you are full of dead man's bones and all uncleanness." "You outwardly appear righteous to men, but inside you are full of hypocrisy and lawlessness." Matthew 23.

His words were far from complimentary. It was Jesus' way of telling them that they were sitting on benches of uselessness and destructiveness, even though they thought they were running the show in a way that pleased God.

29

On one occasion as Jesus was walking on Solomon's porch in the temple, the religious leaders surrounded Him and asked, "If you are really Christ, the Messiah, tell us so plainly and openly." John 10:24 TAB.

Jesus replied, "I have told you so, yet you do not believe me. The very works that I do by the power of my Father and in my Father's name bear witness concerning me. They are my credentials and evidence in support of me. I and my Father are one." John 10:25,30.

Upon hearing this, the Jews reached for rocks to stone Him. According to the Law, the penalty for blasphemy was death by stoning. How blind to the truth they were! They looked at Jesus and saw only a man. They saw the son of Joseph, a carpenter from Nazareth. Their preconceived ideas and their pride prevented them from believing that Jesus was the Promised One, the Son of God. In self-righteous blindness, the leaders who regarded themselves as keepers and teachers of the Law considered His claim to be blasphemy. The Messiah was standing in their midst and they could not recognize Him. In hardness of heart, they could not tolerate Him. They regarded His righteousness to be less than their own. They pronounced Him worthy of death.

In our fundamental churches, it is commonplace to find the self-righteous. With the stipulation of many rules of dos and don'ts, we can easily place ourselves in the limelight by disciplining ourselves to be compliant. Receiving compliments concerning our good efforts and accomplishments feels good. However, we can get trapped into serving the organization, thinking all the while that we are serving the Lord. We can climb the pedestal to the top and look down on others with pride and consternation. We, like the Pharisee who exalted himself before God in the temple, can become proud of our successes and boastful of our accomplishments. Luke 18:11. We can even become proud of our humility. I once heard a man say that he had not committed a single sin in the past four years. Could it be that he was sinning by making such a statement? In acts of self-righteousness the church itself becomes intolerant and unable to demonstrate God's love and forgiveness.

In his book *Born Crucified*, L. E. Maxwell wrote about the many forms of self that are destructive in a believer's life.

"In our service for Christ, self-confidence and self-esteem; in the slightest suffering, self-saving and self-pity; in the least misunderstanding, self-defense and self-vindication; in our station in life, self-seeking and self-centeredness; in the smallest trials, self-inspection and self-accusation; in the daily routine, self-pleasing and self-choosing; in our relationships, self-assertiveness and self-respect; in our education, self-boasting and self-expression; in our desires, self-indulgence and self-satisfaction; in our successes, self-admiration and self-congratulation; in our failures, self-excusing and self-justification; in our spiritual attainments, self-righteousness and self-complacency; in our public ministry, self-reflection and self-glory; in life as a whole, self-love and selfishness."

My late wife was raised in a devoted Christian family that attended a conservative church. In her church, wearing of jewelry was permitted, but wearing of makeup including lipstick was forbidden. I was raised in a devoted Christian family that attended a Mennonite church. At the time of our marriage, wearing some makeup including lipstick was permitted in my church, but wearing jewelry was forbidden. Shortly after we were married, this difference in church rules became a problem between my wife and myself. I felt tremendous pressure for her to comply with the rules of the church and not wear jewelry. My father was the minister. I was on the church Board. One weekday evening, the church Board put pressure on me to have my wife refrain from wearing jewelry as an example for others. Upon going home, I informed her that she could not wear jewelry anymore to our church services.

The following Sunday morning as we were driving to church, I noticed that my wife was wearing a very thin gold chain necklace. So thin that it was barely visible. Swiftly, without saying a word, I reached for the necklace and tore it from her neck. Although this act was done in anger, my religious training forbade a show of anger. So like a good Pharisee, I controlled the tone of my voice when I spoke, "I told you that you can not wear jewelry to our church anymore."

I got some tears in response and the silent treatment for a while. I didn't feel good about the incident, but felt on the other hand that I had acted justly. It was years later, after months of sessions with a

31

Christian psychotherapist, that I shed tears over the incident and asked my wife to forgive me. The self-righteousness in me was slowly dying a painful death and Jesus was setting me free. I was finally moving away from a bench of ineffectiveness.

During my childhood and early teen years, my paternal grandfather was my pastor. I loved him and admired him greatly. As a child, some notes I took from his sermons were dutifully copied from Bible to Bible and are treasures in the Bible I use today. My grandparents were evangelists. It was not enough for them to have a sign on the church lawn advertising that everyone was welcome. They drove across town and ministered to physical and spiritual needs of persons living in depressed housing areas. They witnessed by going door to door. In their simple, nonthreatening way, they were received.

The church began to grow in number. It was natural for persons without a Mennonite heritage to feel uncomfortable sitting among a congregation where persons wore ultra conservative dress and the men sat on one side and the women sat on the other. Nevertheless, some children and youth began attending and later some parents came also. It was a real joy when my grandfather was asked by the parents of these new families to be baptized and become members of the congregation. Upon the completion of catechism classes, my grandfather informed the Bishop that a service needed to be arranged to accommodate their request.

Prior to the Sunday scheduled for the baptismal service, the Bishop came to preach. His sermon went into overtime. As a boy, I kept wondering when he would sit down. He preached about the Biblical pattern of dress. Although certain Bible passages instruct modesty, he incorporated into his sermon the full attire of dress specified for women in the churches under his jurisdiction. Dark dresses with full capes. A mesh covering with two strips of cloth attached at the sides. A black bonnet. Black stockings and black shoes.

Finally, he ended his sermon by saying that until the women and girls seeking baptism and church membership complied with the Biblical standard of dress he had described, baptism and membership would not be granted. The congregation was flabbergasted. I'm certain to this day that the Bishop prided himself in doing his duty as a servant of God. A Pharisee could not have done better.

After the Bishop's departure, my grandparents apologized for his lack of consideration and grace. However, the new families we were hoping would worship with us, found other churches to meet their needs.

Soon afterward, our congregation asked for resignation from the conference to which it belonged and sought membership with another Mennonite conference that offered a more liberal interpretation on the dress issue. Learning to love through our differences rather than permitting differences to divide us is a difficult task. Perhaps as I sat there on that large bench as a child that day, I should have heard a sermon from the Bishop on that subject instead.

In the book *Saints and Snobs*, Marion Jacobsen wrote some words of truth concerning acceptance.

> "Many Christians do not find in their local churches the personal acceptance, love and practical care God intended should be available there. There is no community in all the world that has the dynamic available to the church for accepting and loving people, even the unattractive and undeserving ones. Seldom is their failure to meet the material needs of a poor man in giving him food and clothing, but often there is a failure to accept his person. Fellowship in the early church grew out of shared problems and a sense of responsibility to meet each other's needs. Too often Christians know little about each others' personal needs and feel little responsibility when they do know. People sit side by side in a church pew each week and never get acquainted with each other. They keep their masks firmly in place to give the appearance that they have no personal problems. One seldom has the courage to admit his own deep needs before such a self-sufficient group as the average church group appears. Special relationships where we are fully ourselves are much too rare, as is total acceptance, honest sharing and genuine loving."

During my freshmen year in college, a fellow classmate told me that his bishop had banned him from taking communion and had forbidden him to teach in his church because he had purchased a car that had a radio in it. The car was old and the radio didn't work, but that didn't matter. He didn't consider removal of the radio necessary. He was not permitted to serve in his church due to this petty issue.

There was a woman I knew in my youth who loved the Lord. She was very faithful in attending worship services. Every communion service, however, she observed others participating in the eating of bread and the drinking of the fruit of the vine in remembrance of Jesus' death, but she was forbidden to partake herself.

Years before, she had married a man without knowing that he had been previously married and divorced. He told her about these details after the marriage ceremony. Because she married a divorced man, she was considered an adulteress by the bishop.

She yearned to take communion. Since she could not, communion services were painful for her.

One day as communion Sunday was approaching, she was gazing through her kitchen window while telling the Lord how much she desired to take communion. Suddenly she saw the form of Jesus appear to her in the clouds. Beholding the tender and accepting expression on His face, she knew her Lord understood what she was feeling.

When communion Sunday arrived and the bread and cup were passed, although she could not participate as others did, she partook within her heart. No one could take the joy of that moment from her. She felt satisfied. She felt complete. She knew in her heart that she had remembered her Lord.

Self-righteousness and refusal to reveal our own vulnerability cause us to use our particular list of rules to force the benching of others who fail to satisfy our standards. It is little wonder why this character trait, so common among those professing to be followers of God, was so condemned by Christ.

We live in a world where it is not popular to show grace. It is more appropriate in the mindset of the masses to exhibit toughness and stick up for one's rights. To "be a man". It is far easier to condemn than to forgive.

The very idea of grace seems weak in a world that is aggressive and competitive, and frequently even violent. Grace is not a cheap thing. It cost Jesus His life to make grace available to us. Our God is referred to in the Bible as "the God of all grace". What is this grace of God? It is God's mercy, loving kindness and favor that are given to us, not because we merit it or deserve it in any way. Grace is given to us purely because of who God is and because of His nature of love. God's love, goodness, mercy and kindness are deeper than any human being can ever fathom. Grace is a powerful force, a holy influence that God exerts upon us. A person under the influence of God's grace finds himself under the magnetic force of God's love, drawing him ever closer to Jesus.

Just visualize the picture that Jesus painted for us of the father welcoming his son home; a son who had been rebellious, wasteful, hateful and wicked, and who had radically messed up his life. This father ran to meet his son and embraced him and kissed him; a son who was filthy and smelled terrible because his last place of employment had been in a pig pen where his wages were the food that was fed to the pigs. By giving us this picture of the lost son and the welcoming father, Jesus was showing us the marvelous love and grace of our Heavenly Father, who extends His grace and forgiveness to all who are lost and long to be found. What a thrill it is to be so welcomed by God and to be so totally bathed in His grace!

But to be honest, we need to ask a question. How can it be that we who are so welcomed by God have such difficulty welcoming others? A pastor was washing his car in his driveway while his wife and children were away. Robbie, a twelve-year-old boy who was a new resident, rode up on his bike and asked if he could play with his boys. The pastor explained that his boys weren't home. The pastor had already heard some things about Robbie that weren't very complimentary. But Robbie didn't seem in a hurry to leave. He proceeded to say that he was temporarily living with his aunt because his father was in prison and his mother was always getting drunk. He also told the pastor that he was getting poor grades in school and he got into trouble a lot. Then he blurted out a question, "I know that I'm a bad boy sometimes, but can I play with your boys anyway when they come home?."

The pastor had to swallow rather hard. It was difficult for him to risk extending grace by saying yes to Robbie. But he did grant his permission. He offered grace. And he realized that if he didn't, he would be denying whom he claimed to be; a person who had been changed by the grace of God.

We are so quick to throw our condemning stones at persons who upset us or at persons who get into trouble with the law and those who live morally questionable lives. After all, sin is bad and persons who sin need to be punished. What we often fail to realize is that grace is more powerful to change lives than condemnation.

In the Gospel of John, an account is given in which the teachers of the Law and the Pharisees brutally drag a woman, caught in the act of adultery, to Jesus. Their intention on this occasion was to entrap Jesus in the presence of the people around Him. They were hoping to get Him to openly contradict the Law so they could make a fool of Him. The woman was the bait for the trap. The entire matter reeked of a setup since the Law required that the man involved in this act of adultery be tried as well, and he wasn't even mentioned. John Vawter explains in his book, *Uncommon Graces,* that the religious leaders wanted to put Jesus in a position where He would either have to be lenient on the criminal or lenient on the crime. The Law commanded a punishment of stoning. But it was Jesus' nature to be compassionate. Vawter asks the question, "Would Jesus stand up for the sinner or the standard? Would He be soft on the Law and look like an enemy of the faith, or would He be hard on the lawbreaker and show Himself to be an enemy of the people?"

Jesus, in His wisdom, turned the trap on them. He said, "If any one of you is without sin, let him be the first to throw a stone at her." Slowly, fingers that tightly held stones for throwing relaxed their grip, and one by one the stones fell to the pavement. In turn, from the oldest to the youngest, the accusers walked away because their own hearts condemned them, and they saw their own sins. Somehow, the truth that Jesus always exemplified shone through once again, and they realized that they needed as much of God's grace as the woman they wanted to use as a public example.

Then Jesus asked the woman, "Has no one condemned you?" She replied, "No one, Lord." And Jesus said, "Then neither do I condemn you. Go now and leave your life of sin."

What should be our attitude toward those who fail to meet the standards of righteousness that God has set forth for us to follow? Jesus makes it clear that unless we meet the criteria of being sinless ourselves, we are not justified in pointing the condemning finger at another.

In a story entitled, *The Magic Seeds,* a thief is sentenced to be hung for stealing a small package of meat. Before being taken to the gallows, however, the thief tells the king that he is the only person alive who knows how to plant an apple seed that would grow and bear fruit overnight; and to atone for his crime, he would be willing to teach his secret to the king's court. The king is intrigued and grants the condemned thief this opportunity. The criminal asks for a shovel, a handful of apple seeds and a maiden who has never been kissed.

The next day the king gathers with his advisors to witness the promised event. The thief digs a hole and tells the maiden to pour some water into it. Then he announces that the seeds need to be placed in the hole that was prepared, but he can't do that because the seeds need to be planted by a person who has never stolen a single item, no matter how small or how long ago. Each member of the king's court realizes that they are not qualified to plant the seeds at the risk of the tree not growing to produce fruit overnight. Finally, the thief asks why he is to be singled out and hung when everyone in the king's court has been a thief too.

Well, there is a marked difference between the Law, which includes the commandments of God, and grace. Philip Yancy says in his book, *What's So Amazing About Grace,* "Law magnified disobedience and merely indicated the sickness; while grace brought about the cure." What a difference! Receiving grace is life changing! The Law is impossible for any of us to keep. None of us can achieve the righteousness that God's Law demands. But the good news is that we can choose to receive the grace that God offers to us. The gospel message is that God's grace and love are precious gifts to persons who are undeserving.

The church is first and foremost a community of forgiven and recovering sinners, although we at times have made the church to be something other than this. When the church is the kind of community that God intends it to be, then people in it will not be left without grace and love and forgiveness. The people will know that at the center of their lives together, God is dwelling; for where God is dwelling, there is grace.

John Newton, one of the vilest sinners who ever lived, was converted and became a minister of the gospel of Jesus Christ. He wrote the song, *Amazing Grace,* which has been sung by millions of Christians around the world. Yes! That's what God's grace is. Absolutely, stunningly amazing! And it's free for you and me! Accepting this marvelous gift of God's grace is the answer to leaving the bench of self-righteousness.

*EVERY ONE IS TEMPTED
WHEN HE IS DRAWN AWAY
BY HIS OWN DESIRES
AND ENTICED.
JAMES 1:14.*

*DEARLY BELOVED,
I BEG YOU AS
SOJOURNERS AND PILGRIMS,
ABSTAIN FROM
FLESHLY LUSTS,
WHICH WAR AGAINST
THE SOUL.
I PETER. 2:11.*

Yielding to Lustful Desires

There are numerous accounts in the Bible that warn us as God's children not to yield to lustful temptations. The Bible records many incidences where the people of God gave in to lustful desires. The damage wrought by lustful acts is often extreme and permanent. The benching is severe. Not only does lust bench the offender, it incapacitates others, enclosing victims in envelopes of shame and suffering from injuries received. The lust of one person has the potential to bench many.

> Families are often torn apart.
> Innocent persons are emotionally and psychologically hurt.
> Spouses and children are brutally abused.
> Sometimes persons are even murdered.

Some of the Bible's greatest heroes slew lions and giants and won great battles in the name of Jehovah single-handedly. But, they were reduced to the weakest of men as they lowered their guards and allowed lustful temptations to gain an upper hand.

There was a man named Samson, a deliverer by God's planning. Judges 13-16. The children of Israel had been sorely oppressed at the hands of the Philistines for forty years. In desperation and repentance, they called to Jehovah. In response to their cry, an angel of the Lord appeared to a woman who was barren and told her that she would bear a son who would deliver Israel from the Philistines. Her child was to be a Nazarite unto God from the womb. He was not to drink wine. He was not to eat unclean meat. No razor was to touch his head.

In fulfillment of the promise, Samson was born as the angel had spoken. How mighty he became in strength! One time when the Philistines surrounded his home to take him captive, he slew one thousand of the enemy and put them to flight. He petrified the enemy with fear. Soon they considered him unconquerable in battle.

Then to his parents dismay, Samson announced that he had found a lover in the valley of Sorek in enemy territory. Her name was Delilah. She was beautiful and cunningly seductive. He loved the way she aroused him. He felt he had to have her at any cost. Often he fell asleep in her arms.

41

He lusted for his heathen lover.
He lowered his guard.
He lost sight of his mission.
He became reckless and careless.
He thought he could handle anything.

What did the length of his hair mean anyway? He began to believe that his strength was in his muscles and not in his hair as God had said. All he needed to do when the Philistine soldiers came was to stand up and shake himself and his enemies would flee in terror.

The Philistines threatened to kill Delilah and her family if she failed to discover the secret of Samson's strength. Delilah drew him into her lair when he was tired and weary, and seduced him, seeking the information that could save her from death.

Then the trap was sprung. After much cajoling, Samson revealed that an angel had told his mother the secret of his strength was in the length of his hair. The news was swiftly given to the enemy. Hair was cut. An alarm was sounded. Samson arose from his bed of pleasure too weak to even stand. He was quickly overcome. His eyes were punched out by his enemies. In blindness he was forced to push a grinding stone. The mighty deliverer was benched. Perhaps the bench was his greatest pain. He had failed miserably. Mind torture.

Who would deliver God's people now?
Would God forgive him for his failure?
Would he ever get another chance to fulfill his mission?

Day after day, round and round the millstone he toiled. But a time came when he knew God had forgiven him. His hair was growing. He began to feel stronger. "I mustn't show my strength," he thought. So he feigned weakness. Such darkness. Round and round the millstone. What could he possibly do not being able to see?

Then one day, the young lad that fed him told him about a great party the Lord of the Philistines was having for his elite fighting men on the upper level of the palace. In his mind's view, Samson recalled the two huge pillars that supported the structure. His heart leaped. Here was an opportunity. Would God help him to do the impossible?

He lifted his blind face upward. A desperate prayer burst from his soul. Yes! God would enable him to do it!

In his final hour, Samson moved from the bench that had imprisoned him. Slowly he was led up the palace steps by a little boy. His body was trembling. Yet, strangely, he was overwhelmed with gratitude. His hands found the pillars. He stretched his arms around them. "Run, boy, run," he cried. Then he began to draw the massive columns toward his sides. "God," he cried, "Help me do this." The columns began to buckle and give. Within moments Samson was buried beneath the palace stones. Three thousand of the enemy's best were slain. Israel once again experienced peace. Mission accomplished! Failure. Repentance. Forgiveness. Opportunity. Strength for the miracle.

There was a hero named David. 2 Samuel 11,12. He had slain an armed giant with a sling shot and a pebble. The people sang songs about him and he became Israel's King.

But one day when David should have been leading his army in battle, he was walking along a patio on the roof of his palace. Suddenly his eyes became fixed on a woman taking a bath. What a beautiful woman! How she moved! Not seen by the woman, he continued to observe her, straining his eyes to take in a better view. He began to lust for her. Upon her dressing and disappearance, he retired to his chambers. How pleasurable it was to let his mind feast on what he had seen. "Who was this woman?" "What would it be like to be with her?"

How his lust grew. Soon it became uncontrollable. It flowed like an avalanche. With some detective work, he found that her name was Bathsheba. He summoned her to his palace and seduced her. After all, he was the King. He deserved the kingdom's best. How he enjoyed her! It didn't seem to matter to him that she was another man's wife.

Then the situation of his adulterous relationship with Bathsheba became complicated. She informed him that she was pregnant. What a predicament! This had to remain a secret. But how? Soon he had a plan and he put it into action. He called Uriah, Bathsheba's husband, home from the battle, made him drunk and told him to go home to his wife, hoping that Uriah would believe that the child was his. Uriah, however, in faithfulness to his comrades in the heat of battle, and in devotion to his King, slept on the palace steps. He didn't see his wife that night.

When David learned of this, his mind worked evil swiftly. He sent Uriah back to the battle with a note to his commanding officer to fix things so Uriah would be killed in a skirmish with the enemy. Soon word was sent to David that Bathsheba's husband had been killed. After Bathsheba finished her mourning, David called for her. She became his wife. The cover-up had worked to perfection. Or had it?

Soon the prophet Nathan stood before David with word that Jehovah was sorely displeased with what he had done. David was found worthy of death, but was informed that his life would be spared. However, the prophet said the child Bathsheba was carrying would die. David retreated to the bench where he spent his darkest hours. Soon all in Israel learned what he had done. In shame and disgrace, he struggled to find forgiveness and cleansing. His fasting and crying before the Lord that the innocent child could live was to no avail. On the seventh day the child died. David achieved no more heroic acts. Because his hands had shed innocent blood, he was denied his greatest personal ambition to build a temple for the Lord. He could leave the bench to write psalms and praise his God for his loving kindness, mercy and forgiveness. He could gather some materials for building the house for God. But he could not begin construction of the temple. That honor would wait for another.

During the years of my father's pastorate while I was still in school, our church always had a large summer Bible School. A major effort was made on these occasions to get children in the neighborhood and beyond to attend. The church bus would often be filled as it made its rounds. One summer, several children from a large family came to the Bible School meetings. Their prior religious exposure had been minimal. Through follow-up visitation, the parents began to attend the morning worship service with their children. We were encouraged by their attendance and were praying for their salvation.

However, after a while, the family stopped coming to the services without an explanation. Visiting in their home didn't provide a reasonable answer either. But sometime later, we learned what had happened. Their seventeen year old daughter looked a lot like her mother. She was attractive in appearance. From all indications, it seemed that she had a good relationship with her parents, but the father had gradually acquired a lustful eye for his daughter. This lust burned within him. One time when he was with her at home, he sexually abused her and she became pregnant.

Soon the daughter and her father became bitter enemies. Their prior love turned into hatred. The family was torn apart when it became known that the daughter was pregnant with her father's child. Her father attempted to justify his wrongdoing by explaining that he wanted to teach her about sex so she would protect herself from boys who would try to use her.

The pregnancy forced the daughter to drop out of school. It also obligated her to testify against her father who later was imprisoned. By God's grace, after years of pain and working through the hurt, the family became reunited.

Much brokenness results from abusive sexual acts that are driven by raw lust. Several moments have the potential to wipe out lifetimes. Often the hatred that results exceeds the intensity of the love that existed before.

God is a Master at creating good from bad. He never fails in His forgiveness. He never leaves us alone. He leads us from despair and guilt. He schools us. He strengthens us. In the sunshine of His love, He enables us to leave our benches behind.

The Apostle Paul emphasized very strongly to the Christians at Corinth the importance of learning from the experiences of our fathers. He wrote to them about the Israelites on their journey from Egypt to Canaan. I Cor. 10:1-11.

> "All our fathers were under the cloud." (God's guidance).
> "All passed through the sea." (God's deliverance).
> "All were baptized unto Moses." (Identified with the work and purpose of their leader and were consecrated unto God).
> "All ate the same spiritual meat." (Spiritual life).
> "All drank the same spiritual drink." (Purification) Heb. 9:22.

"But," Paul writes:

> "They lusted after evil things."
> "They fell."
> "They were destroyed by serpents and the destroyer."
> "They were overthrown in the wilderness."

45

So he warns them:

"Don't be idolaters."
"Don't commit fornication."
"Don't tempt Christ."
"Don't murmur."

And he continues, "Now all these things happened unto them for examples, and they are written for our admonition."

This "but" Paul wrote about is a sad commentary of man's continual inclination to do evil. We do well to review the record and take heed. Taking heed will prevent our stumbling and benching. Perhaps, even our destruction.

A Chaplain I know who works for the Bureau of Prisons told me about an incident that disappointed and pained him greatly. During his seminary years, he had a very close friend. Their families fellowshipped together and enjoyed each other's friendship as well. His friend was very talented in music. He had a beautiful singing voice. He had a tremendous ability to learn languages and readily learned Hebrew. After seminary, he got a job as a musical director of a local church.

One night about a year and a half later, the Chaplain picked up his telephone and called to see how his friend was doing. His wife answered the phone, her voice cracking and broken. As soon as she realized who was calling, she began sobbing uncontrollably. After a while she related through tears that police had just come and handcuffed her husband and took him away. Her three small children were all standing by her crying.

Her husband had become involved in an immoral act with another person in the community and was later sentenced. He is presently serving a twenty-year sentence in a county jail.

Confession and repentance of our sins is always the way back to a right standing with God. These are the keys to unlock God's forgiveness and cleansing. How wonderful it is to know that there is a balm in Gilead to heal those who are weary in soul. True repentance is birthed in a desire to be saved and separated from our sin, not just to be separated from the trouble our sin gets us into.

When I was a teenager, I remember sharing my testimony with a seventeen-year old girl. After reviewing with her the plan of salvation, I asked her if she would like to forsake her life of sin and accept the salvation Jesus died to give her. Tears were streaming down her face. I felt certain that she would say yes. I'll never forget her reply. Through her tears she looked at me sadly and said, "I can't do that. I like my sin too much."

So we make our choices concerning the matter of personal salvation from the guilt, penalty and power of the sins that master us. Choices for bondage or freedom. Choices for fleeting pleasure or lasting joy. Choices for life or choices for death.

No one on earth can deny that King David made a superb choice when he cried out to God the prayer of Psalm 57:

> "Have mercy upon me, O God. Wash me thoroughly from my iniquity, and cleanse me from my sin. For I acknowledge my transgressions and my sin is ever before me. Purge me with hyssop, and I shall be clean: wash me, and I shall be whiter than snow. Create in me a clean heart, O God; and renew a right spirit within me. Restore unto me the joy of thy salvation."

A decisive choice. Beautiful. Unregrettable. A choice that will always put us back in the game.

47

Frank H Leaman

*WHOEVER DRINKS
OF THE WATER THAT I SHALL
GIVE HIM
WILL NEVER THIRST.
BUT THE WATER
THAT I SHALL GIVE HIM
WILL BECOME IN HIM
A FOUNTAIN OF WATER
SPRINGING UP
INTO EVERLASTING LIFE.
JOHN 4:14.*

Low Self-Esteem

One of the greatest liberating convictions that we can acquire is the awareness that the only opinion about us that really matters belongs to God. Thus, we learn to accept ourselves because God accepts us and loves us as His children. Through the realization of God's acceptance of us comes the ability for us to accept ourselves, so there is no need to strive to gain the praise of others or to become shut down by the rejection of others. Feelings of inferiority, inadequacy and low self-worth do not need to become a force that ultimately puts us on the bench, chained by a sense of utter worthlessness.

However, in the grind of life's circumstances, we frequently devaluate ourselves. The world is full of good people who feel inadequate and inferior. Innate within us are compelling needs to be loved, accepted and to feel satisfaction in our accomplishments. It is our nature to go to virtually any length to have these needs met. When dealt a continuous chain of messages that confirm disapproval and rejection in the form of a negative reply, a cutting put-down, an unfair comparison or an impatient response, the lack of appreciation and disrespect solidifies feelings of worthlessness. Failure to win the approval of others breeds feelings of desperation and despair. Nothing is as cruel as the rejection and denial of love. Nothing can dull the searing pain that results from feeling unwanted. The emotional torment causes improper behavior to intensify. Then there is more condemnation. More anguish of soul. More failure and punishment of self. Crushing feelings of inferiority that make escape seem hopeless.

Dr. David Seamands in his book *Healing for Damaged Emotions,* mentions four ways that low self-esteem brings defeat and failure into our lives. Low self-esteem:

> Paralyzes our potential.
> Destroys our dreams.
> Ruins our relationships.
> Sabotages our Christian service.

He says, "The trouble is that low self-esteem robs God of marvelous opportunities to show off His power and ability through

51

our weaknesses. Nothing sabotages Christian service more than thinking so little of ourselves that we don't give God a chance."

When we feel that we don't measure up, we either suffer from an inferiority complex which makes us feel inadequate and injects within us self-depreciation, or we suffer from a perfection complex which makes us feel as though we should have done better than we did and drives us to self-condemnation. Thus, persons who cannot be satisfied with their performance, always berate themselves and feel inferior. It isn't possible for them to feel good about themselves because their sense of value and worth is dependent upon what measuring up means to them. The trap of low self-esteem and poor self-worth springs and tenaciously holds them in captivity. But hope for release is graciously offered by our Savior.

One day Jesus left Jewish territory to meet someone - a woman of poor reputation who lived in Samaria. John 4. A targeted woman. A part of the scum in the town of Sychar. Men used her, abused her and then deserted her. Over and over again, she felt painful rejection. Alone again. Love given, but not returned. And the women of her town knifed her plight with their hateful gossip. "Did you hear? Her fifth husband left her. She's a wretch. It's impossible for her to keep a man. There's no hope for her. She's a slut."

How it all hurt! Coming from so many directions. How could she escape it? How could she change things for the better? She was who she was.

She was a desperate clinger. Her insecurity forced her to have a critical dependency on men. She would cling harder and harder until her man would break free and run. Men dumped women in those days. Women had no authority to break a marriage relationship.

Lonely evenings of plastic smiles and shallow laughter. Guilt. Shame. Self-blame. Isolation from family and neighbors. Gloom. Despair. A promise made. A promise broken. Out on the street again. Where was God? She wondered if she could ever find Him? Could He ever find her? Did God care at all about how she had been treated? These were the questions that tore at the heart of the woman of Sychar.

Now her face was lined with age beyond her years. Her steps toward the well were wearisome and slow. Even though her water jar was empty, it weighted her shoulders down. Her heart was heavy. Life was bitter. It stank. At least she was going to the well at noon when she could be alone. The women who shunned her went for water in the evening. This was their social time to talk about things that had happened during the day. The other women made her feel unwelcome. How she despised their condemning glances!

Suddenly someone was speaking to her. "Give me a drink of water from the well," He requested. His voice sounded so kind. It puzzled her. Cautiously she raised her head and gazed at the expression on His face. There was a tenderness about it. But why? Something was weird about this man being at the well. He was a Jew. What was He doing in Samaria? The Jews despised Samaritans. They called people like her dogs.

She had to know. Dare she ask Him? She decided to risk it. "Why do you ask me, a Samaritan woman, to draw water for you? You are a Jew."

Jesus replied, "If you knew who I am and knew about the living water I can give you, you would ask me for a drink."

She took her time and pondered His strange statement. He seemed so sincere. So unthreatening. So genuine. Almost reverently she asked, "What is living water?"

Jesus knew He had aroused her interest. He answered, "Whoever drinks of the water I give will never thirst again. It will be like a well of water springing up inside unto everlasting life."

She knew that whatever He meant, she wanted what He had to offer. Didn't He say whoever? But a Samaritan woman? How could it be? Then her spirit fell as she thought, "He doesn't know how messed up my life is. If He did, He wouldn't be giving me His attention."

But she couldn't let such an opportunity pass. So she blurted out, "Sir, give me this water."

Unknown to her, the sinful life she was living was no secret to Jesus. He replied, "Go home and get your husband. Bring him to me and I will tell you."

A freight train load of frustrating thoughts started racing through her brain. She panicked. What could she tell Him? "Of all things, why did He ask me to do that?", she thought. She decided to simply say, "I don't have a husband."

Jesus replied, "I know that. You have had five husbands and the man you are living with now is not your husband."

She was stunned. She couldn't believe what she had heard. How did He know about her life's tragedies? She looked at Him in utter amazement. It seemed like His eyes were piercing deep into her soul. What kind of man was this? She studied His face, then slowly began to relax. His face didn't show disdain. It didn't show disappointment. He wasn't turning to leave her. She had never had a conversation so intensely moving with anyone. His manner gave her a sense that He actually loved her. Not the way other men had loved her. Not a "use you" kind of love, but a "help you" kind of love. She felt her heart pounding within her breast. Finally she said, "You must be a prophet. I know that a Messiah is to come that will tell us all things."

Then Jesus revealed to her His true identity. He stated slowly and clearly in a way that she couldn't miss the awesome truth, "I am the Christ."

The promised Messiah gracing her with His presence. Bathing her with His love. What a glorious moment! She thought she was in Heaven. Yes. Indeed. He was the Messiah! She believed Him. In an instant of time she took a drink of the living water. She became transformed.

> Her weight of sin and guilt suddenly disappeared.
> Her heartache gave way to rejoicing.
> Her loneliness and depression were banished by a new hope.
> She was accepted by the Messiah, the Christ.
> She was now a person of worth who enjoyed a new identity in Christ.

What wonderful news! News this tremendous and exciting - news this life changing had to be shared! In her new found joy, she abruptly spun around. Leaving her water pot sitting on the well, she broke into a run. Minutes later she arrived at her village. Between her pants for air, she shouted, "Come and see a man who told me all the things I ever did. He is the Christ."

Her neighbors were shocked. What had come over this woman of ill repute? This woman who eluded them at every opportunity. This woman who used to be so unhappy. What made her so radiant now? They had to know. So they dropped what they were doing and hastened with her to the well.

Jesus was waiting for them. Soon He heard their chattering voices in the distance. He had captivated the curiosity of the town by giving a drink of His living water to one of their most disregarded citizens.

Many believed Him. They begged Him to stay with them and teach them. He did. His living water completely satisfied all who opened their thirsty hearts to Him.

In his book *Healing Life's Hurts*, Ron Lee Davis wrote, "We're all crippled. We all have feelings of inadequacy in our lives, and these feelings hold us back from being everything God wants us to be. God never intended us to feel beaten down by the past or paralyzed by a sense of inferiority. Rather, He calls us to make the healing choice for the hurt of inferiority - the choice to dwell on His truth about ourselves."

We, with our feelings of low self-worth, need to value the constant approval of God over the conditional approval of people. The Good News is Christ's unconditional love that never fails. Redeeming love spilled the blood of Jesus that flowed from the cross. It flowed in an eternal stream to cleanse and to forgive. To heal our sinful hearts and quench our thirst. And in a real sense, the blood of Christ continues to flow to set us free from the chains of low self-esteem and enables us to serve the living God.

At the cross is certain release for the guilt, the power and the penalty of our sin. It is the only place in all of God's universe where we become so surrounded by His perfect acceptance and unconditional love that our broken selves are made whole. We realize our worth even in our imperfection because Jesus Christ considered us worth dying for. He is the healer of all our wounds.

The apostle Paul wrote in his letter to Titus, "Not by works of righteousness which we have done, but according to His mercy He saved us, by the washing of regeneration, and the renewing of the Holy Spirit, whom He poured out on us abundantly through Jesus Christ our Savior; that being justified by His grace, we should be made heirs according to the hope of eternal life." Titus 3:5-7.

Robert McGee stated God's answer for us in his book *The Search for Significance* as follows:

> "If we base our self-worth on our ability to meet standards, we will try to compensate by either avoiding risks or trying to succeed no matter what the cost. Either way, failure looms as a constant enemy. But God has set us free from the fear of failure! He has given us a secure self-worth totally apart from our ability to perform. We have

been justified, placed in right standing before God through Christ's death on the cross to pay for our sins. But God didn't stop with our forgiveness. He also granted us the very righteousness of Christ! By imputing righteousness to us, God attributes Christ's worth to us. The moment we accept Christ, God no longer sees us as condemned sinners. Instead, we are forgiven and Christ's righteousness is granted to us, and God sees us as completely righteous and in right standing with Him. Therefore, we are fully pleasing to Him. Our relationship with God, our security and our self-worth are not earned by our own efforts. They are obtained by grace through faith."

Our identity in Christ is the key to wholeness. This state of wholeness and meaning in life doesn't hinge on what we have done or haven't done, or what we possess or don't possess. It hinges on who we are - the children of God. Self-worth is an identity issue. Accepted by God and clothed in the righteousness of Christ Jesus, we view ourselves as persons in process and move forward in loving and serving our God and others as we are able. God will replace our weaknesses with His strength as we dedicate our abilities to Him and seek to use them for His glory. This is our sole purpose for living - living life as the children of God and serving Him with all that we are. Self-esteem is essential to fulfill God's intentions for our lives. The bench and feelings of low self-worth can be left behind. Praise God for His unfailing love and acceptance of us who indeed are all unworthy of such mercy and grace.

We all need to come to Jesus, the Living Water, as repentant sinners. He died for us, enduring the pain of Calvary's cross. That's how much He loves us. And His promise is to forgive, pardon and cleanse every sinner who comes to Him.

Have you met Jesus at your well of loneliness, at your well of thirst, at your well that has been emptied by the curse of sin? The Good News of the Gospel of Christ is the living water that quenches the deepest thirst of our souls. It is pure love flowing from the very heart of God that reaches to embrace and fill all persons, even the lonely and the despised and rejected. This is God's gift to us. What a gift it is! In Christ alone is our way to wholeness. We all need to meet Jesus at the well. The refreshment and strength we are blessed with there, lifts us from our benches of low self-esteem. We discover that our worthiness is in Christ. In Him we are welcomed into God's family.

Frank H Leaman

*WOE TO YOU WHO ARE
AT EASE IN ZION.
WHO LIE ON BEDS OF IVORY,
STRETCH OUT
ON YOUR COUCHES,
AND EAT THE LAMBS
FROM THE FLOCK.
AMOS 6:1, 4.*

Frank H Leaman

Complacency

As children of the kingdom of God we are called to participate in a race to the finish. The Apostle Paul with deliberate certainty ran his race to the completion of the course and encouraged many along the way to continue running. To run hard. To run well.

> "Do you not know that those who run in a race all run, but one receives the prize. Run that you might obtain it." I Corinthians 9:24.
> "Let us lay aside every weight, and the sin which so easily ensnares us, and let us run with endurance the race that is set before us." Hebrews 12:1.

In a race, no runner casually stands up from the starting block at the crack of the starter's gun and begins to leisurely walk down the track while the other runners are straining for top performance. Neither do any runners look for a place along the course to sit down and rest a while.

So why in the race of living, loving and serving one another do so many of God's people stop running? We are all very familiar with the remarks persons make who choose to shirk their duties.

> I need a rest.
> I've done enough.
> Let someone else take up the slack.
> I'm retiring.
> I need a change.
> I need some time to enjoy life.

Running the race for our Lord is not a duty. It is a privilege. It is a lifelong commitment. Not a matter of convenience.

Who said the race would be easy? Not Jesus. He set His face like a flint toward Jerusalem where He would be brutally tortured and crucified. Not Paul. He was beaten with whips and rods and thrown into jails time and again for proclaiming the Good News. He was even stoned and left for dead. He suffered hunger and thirst and exposure to cold.

But Paul didn't allow threatening, unfavorable and painful circumstances to keep him from pressing toward the finish line. In his difficulties he saw opportunities. Opportunities to pray. To sing. To witness. To write. If any Christian ever would have been entitled to rest on his laurels it would have been Paul. But he didn't. He kept on running.

I love the admonition Paul wrote in Hebrews chapter 12.

> "Looking unto Jesus, the author and finisher of our faith; who for the joy that was set before him endured the cross, despising the shame, and has sat down at the right hand of the throne of God. For consider him that endured such hostility from sinners against himself, lest you become weary and discouraged in your souls. You have not yet resisted to bloodshed, striving against sin." Hebrews 12:2-4.

What a message! "Consider Him."
And I love the proclamation Paul wrote to the church at Philippi.

> "I can do all things through Christ who strengthens me." Philippians 4:13.

There are times when we feel like giving up. When the way becomes difficult and we feel exhausted. But we are not entitled to quit. And sleeping on the job is not an acceptable solution. Christ will supply the grace and strength we need to do His bidding for the asking.

It's so easy to succumb to time out like the disciples did in the Garden of Gethsemane. Mark 26:36-41. Jesus in sheer agony asked His followers to pray. He told them that His soul was sorrowful even unto death. But they fell asleep. Not once, but twice.

As disciples of Christ, we need to make intentional commitments to be faithful. To remain focused. To be willing to do the tasks at hand even when our flesh complains.

In his book *Waiting, Finding Hope When God Seems Silent*, Ben Patterson tells about the last sixteen years of ministry of Dr. Charles McCoy. Dr. McCoy was pastoring a Baptist church in Oyster Bay, New York, when at age seventy-two he was mandated by his denomination to retire. Just prior to leaving his congregation, he met a pastor from India who invited him to come to India sometime to preach in his church. Dr. McCoy prayed about it and felt led to go to India.

He booked a one-way passage to Bombay. He arrived in Bombay only to discover that his luggage had been lost. Later his wallet and passport were stolen. Then he found missionaries who informed him that the Indian pastor he met was still in the United States and was planning to remain there indefinitely. All advice offered to him was discouraging.

Not knowing what to do, he decided to visit the mayor of Bombay to obtain permission to preach. He knew he had come to India to preach. When the mayor noted from his business card that he had earned seven university degrees including two Ph. D's, he was so impressed that he invited Dr. McCoy to attend a tea. There he met the director of India's West Point, the National Defense Academy at Poona. This man asked Dr. McCoy to preach at the Academy. Thus was launched sixteen more years of ministry in India and Hong Kong. He died in a hotel in Calcutta at the age of eighty-eight while resting for a meeting where he was to preach that evening.

Just like the Apostle Paul. Running to the finish line. Many said, "Quit. You're too old. Retire in Florida."

But God's instructions were to go to India and preach. And he did.

When I was a child, one of my favorite Bible stories was the story of Gideon and his devoted army of three hundred. Judges 6-7. But I don't recall ever being told the end of the story. The story, as I was told it, always ended with the Midianites smiting themselves in raw terror in the blackness of the night while attempting to escape from the army of the Lord and Gideon.

Following the victory of one hundred twenty thousand slain, the men of Israel said to Gideon, "Rule over us for you have delivered us from the hand of Midian."

But Gideon replied, "I will not rule over you. The Lord shall rule over you." Judges 8:23. He refused a position of lordship among them. For that he is to be commended.

However, he made a decision to rest on his laurels. He collected the golden earrings that the Israelites had taken from the defeated enemy. Eight hundred fifty troy ounces of gold. Then he made an ephod of gold and set it up in his city. The trophy became a snare and all Israel went "a whoring after it."

With the gifts the men of Israel gave him, Gideon became very wealthy. He married many wives and had seventy sons. It seems that he gradually took on an epicurean philosophy. Eat, drink and be merry. No more visitations by angels. No more daring assignments.

A tremendous opportunity was lost. By the time Gideon died, Israel had forgotten "the Lord their God who had delivered them out of the hands of all their enemies." Judges 8:34.

We need to be careful that the blessings we receive in life don't cause a shift of our devotion from our Lord to the blessings. Just before the children of Israel entered the Promised Land, they were given these words of admonition.

> "When you have eaten and are full, then you shall bless the Lord your God for the good land which he has given you. Beware that you do not forget the Lord your God by not keeping his commandments, and his judgments, and his statutes, which I command you today. Lest when you have eaten and are full, and have built beautiful houses and dwell in them; And when your herds and your flocks multiply, and your silver and your gold are multiplied, and all that you have is multiplied; when your heart is lifted up, and you forget the Lord your God who brought you out of the land of Egypt, from the house of bondage." Deuteronomy 8:10-14.

In his book *The Heart of the Faith*, Gary Demarest speaks about commitment as an essential element of our faith.

> "Perhaps for those of us in the developed countries, the greatest barrier to genuine commitment is our relative affluence. We feel we have worked too long and hard to get what we have to hazard losing it. To commit to One who affirms that 'it is more blessed to give than to receive' (Acts 20:35) does not easily fit into our categories. We prefer our material and physical security above all else, and we play it safe all around.

Jesus certainly made the issue clear to the rich young ruler: 'Sell everything you have and give to the poor... Then come, follow me'. Luke 18:22. While there is probably no need to apply this imperative to every person universally as though it were the eleventh commandment, those of us basking in the midst of affluence must take a good look at the substance of the issue involved.

In the priorities of his wealth and power, this young man was still seeking for the meaning of 'eternal life'. The essence of life was lacking, although he certainly had every reason to celebrate success. He had practiced traditional morality to perfection, but it wasn't enough. The diagnosis of Jesus was direct and to the point.

The young man's basic problem was his unwillingness to commit to anything that was not in his best interests as measured from the standpoint of material security and well-being. This is the potential tragedy of affluence. It has a way of becoming a pseudo-faith in a way of life."

So we are duly warned against becoming complacent. We are to continually honor and serve our Lord in all circumstances. There is no "At ease" command in the lives of believers. To be at ease is to be on the bench and out of the game.

What a blessing it is to read about Anna, the prophetess, in Luke chapter two. A widow woman eighty-four years old who "departed not from the temple, but served God with fasting and prayer night and day." Pressing onward to the finish line. What a noble runner!

Frank H Leaman

DIRECT MY STEPS BY YOUR WORD, AND LET NO INIQUITY HAVE DOMINION OVER ME.
PSALM 119:133.

Frank H Leaman

Guilt

Guilt is the most destructive emotion we can experience. It's tentacles squeeze from us our self-respect and dry our spirits. Past failures cause us to interpret present failures as confirmation of our worthlessness. We become caught in a cyclone of despair, feeling unloved, unwanted and unaccepted. Guilt leads to depression. And often the depression breeds habitual failure. A cycle develops that traps us in aloneness. Attention becomes focused on our repeated failures until the ability to cope is suffocated and self-affliction takes over. Guilt piles upon guilt.

> It shackles and binds us.
> It robs us of hope.
> It invites despair.
> It envelops us in shame.

By repeating our failures, our very life becomes riveted to them. Gradually, we become convinced that we cannot change. We see no way out of our dilemma. Our failures consume our memory until all we can recall about ourselves is bad. The emotional trauma caused by failure can lead to the destruction of self and others. Abuse, sexual promiscuity and experimentation with drugs often result. Sometimes persons are even driven to suicide.

When feelings of guilt are not eradicated early, we lose the ability to respect ourselves because our behavior reflects what we think to be true about ourselves. It becomes necessary for us to become masters of deception. In our efforts to deceive others, we eventually can become strangers to our own selves. By focusing on our failures, we lose sight of God's intent for us in the future.

Judas no doubt had pretended to be a true follower of Jesus for a long time. He learned what to say and how to act to gain acceptance from the others who followed Jesus. He was shrewd. But in time, his true colors could no longer be concealed. His deceptive mask fell and the hardness of his heart was exposed. He betrayed his Master for thirty pieces of silver. Matthew 26:15.

Perhaps he felt he was doing a good thing, thinking that the confrontation would force Jesus to crush the opposition and establish

His kingdom. Every wrongdoer seeks justification for his actions. Whatever Judas thought, it doesn't seem that he was prepared to see Jesus die on the cross. That sight invoked an unbearable burden of guilt upon him. It so weighted him down that he got a rope and found a tree. He ended his life in the blackness of night. A bitter night. A wasted life.

In his book *Emotions: Can You Trust Them*, Dr. James Dobson wrote about guilt as a painful emotion.

> "Few human emotions are as distressing and painful as feelings of guilt and personal disapproval. When at a peak of intensity, self-condemnation gnaws on the conscious mind by day and invades the dreams by night. Since the voice of the conscience speaks from inside the human mind, we can not escape its unrelenting abuse for our mistakes, failures and sins. For some particularly vulnerable individuals, an internal taskmaster is on the job from early morning until late at night - screaming accusations at his tormented victim. Hospitals for the emotionally disturbed are filled with such patients who have been unable to meet their own expectations and are now broken with self-blame and even personal hatred."

So it was with Judas. Raw searing pain. A self-blame and hatred of self unto death.

When Jesus was arrested and led away by the Roman guard, another disciple followed at a safe distance, hiding in the shadows, wanting to know what was happening, but fearing that the fate of his Lord might become his own. Peter, the man who had declared several hours before, "Lord, I am ready to go with you, both into prison and to death," was overcome with fear. Luke 22:33.

While Jesus was being incarcerated in the priest's house, Peter became cold and went to warm himself by a fire burning in the hall. A woman remarked that Peter had been with the man who had just been arrested. Peter denied that he knew Jesus.

Yet another claimed that Peter had been with Jesus. He denied it again. Then a third person charged that Peter was a Galilean and was a follower of Jesus. Peter vehemently denied his acquaintance with Jesus a third time with cursing and swearing. Then the cock crowed.

Painful memory shock drew Peter's mind to the words Jesus had spoken to him earlier, "The cock shall not crow this day before you will thrice deny that you know me." Peter went out into the night, a solitary man crushed by guilt, feeling severed from God and man. He wept bitterly. Fear had incapacitated him. He had denied the very purpose he had found for his own existence. He had denied his Lord. No doubt he too thought about using a rope and a tree.

It is difficult to imagine the night of horror Peter endured. Excruciating guilt. Unbearable shame. He gave himself scores of kicks and blows. His mind was filled with agonizing questions and unresolved answers.

Could there ever be forgiveness for him?
Would he ever be given another chance?
Would he be strong enough to tell the truth if another chance came?
Would he ever have enough faith to overcome such fear?
What kind of a cheap coward was he?
Could he ever face Jesus again?

Peter was on the bench. For a man of action it was a terrible feeling. A horribly degrading experience.

But God's grace finds all who desire to be found. A day came for Peter when he was able to talk to Jesus by the sea shore face to face. John 21:15-17.

He felt undeserving.
He felt uncomfortable.
He was still ashamed.
He was still hurting inside.

Even so, Jesus asked him, "Peter, do you love me with a pure and perfect love?" Jesus used the Greek word, agape, for love here. A perfect love.

Peter replied that he loved Jesus, but his love was not a perfect love. Jesus repeated His question and Peter repeated his answer.

Then Jesus asked, "Peter, do you love me with a love that isn't perfect?" Jesus used the Greek word, phileo, for love in his third question. An imperfect love.

Peter replied, "Jesus, you know that I love you with a love that isn't perfect." Peter had told the truth, no longer bragging about having a perfect, unswerving devotion to Jesus. His head hung downward in an expression of his shame.

Can't you hear Jesus saying, "Peter, look at me?" When Peter's gaze was fixed on Jesus, he heard the sweet words of acceptance, "Feed my sheep."

Suddenly there was a new purpose for living. Jesus understood the problem he had with an imperfect love, but was willing to love him perfectly anyway. Jesus, his Lord, had assigned him a task to do the work of the kingdom anyway. He was back in the game. The tears of his soul pain gave way to joy. In the work of the kingdom he still counted for something. He was forgiven!

A friend of mine felt called of God to be a minister of the Gospel. He and his wife were looking forward to serving the Lord as missionaries. However, during his senior year of studies, a transgression he committed was discovered and he was expelled. When he needed grace the most, it was denied him. He became captivated by an enormous load of guilt and shame. The trauma of the situation compounded with an inferiority complex that he had suffered since childhood, caught in a whirlpool of depression that almost destroyed him. In an abyss of rejection and loneliness, he became victimized with a slavery mentality that eroded his emotional strength and eclipsed his self worth.

Eventually his marriage was broken by divorce. Even after years of counseling and psychotherapy, some wounds of rejection still remain. Does God still love him? With a perfect love. Do I still love him? Very much. Does he love himself? He is still learning how. And who knows what great things God will yet accomplish through his life?

In this age of grace, God's spirit is faithful in finding us in our places of hiding, convicting us of sin and drawing us to the Father who remains eager to pardon. The problem of broken fellowship lies at the doorstep of humanity. God has pursued us, the crown of His creation and the apple of His eye. He revealed Himself in flashes of lightning, in mountains of smoke, in the parting of the sea, in a pillar of fire by night and a cloud over the desert by day, in the voices of prophets, in a babe divinely born in a manger, in the Son of God sent among us to show us the Father and demonstrate His love, in Jesus

Christ giving of Himself in death on the cross, and in the resurrection of Jesus from the tomb. Praise God! He has the answer to our burdens of guilt. The forgiveness of our sins. When we sin, the solution is not to run from God and sit on a bench of guilt. The solution is to run toward God, seeking His forgiveness and restoration. The shackles of guilt will be broken. We can get back into the game.

Frank H Leaman

**PRIDE AND ARROGANCE
AND THE EVIL WAY
AND THE PERVERSE
MOUTH I HATE. PROV. 8:13.**

**PRIDE GOES BEFORE
DESTRUCTION,
AND A HAUGHTY SPIRIT
BEFORE A FALL. PROV. 16:18.**

Frank H Leaman

Pride

It is not uncommon for pride to bench God's people. Jesus included pride in the list of sins He mentioned that come from the heart of man. Jeremiah reminded the children of Israel, "The pride of your hearts has deceived you." Jeremiah 49:16 NIV. Pride, like the sin of self-righteousness, can place us on benches of uselessness and destructiveness. It's power makes us think that we are big enough to challenge the ways of our Creator. It has a way of blinding us to our weaknesses and needs.

Pride gave birth to Lucifer's boasting as recorded by the prophet Isaiah.

> "I will ascend into heaven,
> I will exalt my throne above the stars of God,
> I will sit upon the mount of the congregation,
> and I will be like the most high." Isaiah 14:13,14.

God's sentence of judgment against Lucifer was, "You shall be brought down to hell." Pride is a deadly sin that cannot be tolerated in God's kingdom.

Nebuchadnezzar, the king of ancient Babylon, was not considered one of God's people, but was accountable to God as he had witnessed the miraculous salvation of the three Hebrew boys and the interpretation of his dreams by Daniel. As he walked upon the great wall he had built around Babylon and gazed upon its magnificent buildings, his heart swelled in pride. He declared, "This is the great Babylon that I have built by the might of my power and for the honor of my majesty." Daniel 4:30.

While he was still speaking, God said from heaven, "To you it is spoken. The kingdom is departed from you. They shall drive you from men, and your dwelling shall be with the beasts of the field, and seven times shall pass over you, until you know that the Most High rules in the kingdoms of men, and gives it to whomever He chooses." And so it was. Nebuchadnezzar became insane and was driven from his palace by his servants.

Then, following seven years in the field, Nebuchadnezzar's mind returned to him again. His kingdom was given back to him and his lips were filled with praise to the God of Heaven and earth to whom he owed his life and his accomplishments.

The wrong in pride is claiming for one's self the credit that is God's. Pride fails to give God His place in the universe that He has created. It is listed in the Bible among the sins that God hates.

The elder brother in the story of the Prodigal son also had a problem with pride. He was self-centered. There was no doubt that he thought he was better than his brother. He was superior. In his eyes he had done everything right. He deserved the party instead of his good-for-nothing, waste-it-all brother. His pride and envy benched him from the celebration. He was robbed of the joy and merriment. Worse yet, his view of his father became distorted. He felt his father was foolish, unfair and unjust. His father was showing love for another that he could not understand. In defiance, he shut off his father's love.

Pride does that in us.

It breeds envy.
It doesn't understand love.
It blinds us to our own imperfections.
It deceives us into thinking we are better than we are.
It causes us to defy our Maker.

When I was serving as the Sunday School Superintendent in the church my father was pastoring, the woman who had the responsibility for the church library frequently missed services. Her husband was an alcoholic. Problems at home sometimes prevented her attendance. When the next elections were held for persons to assume positions of leadership in the church, another woman who was faithful in attendance was selected to be the librarian.

The following Sunday, I told the congregation that a new librarian had been elected and she asked me to announce that the library would be open <u>every</u> Sunday. I did not realize that the woman just replaced was present that morning and that my statement offended her.

However, I found out several weeks later that she was deeply hurt and angered by my statement. In my pride, I felt I had no responsibility. I had not intentionally meant to offend her. I had just mentioned factual information. After all, the new librarian had asked me to inform the congregation that the library would be open every Sunday. I delayed any apology.

Finally, my mother spoke to me about the matter and asked me to speak with the woman I had offended. She made it clear to me that healing could take place only if I admitted guilt and asked for forgiveness. What? I was to do that? Yes. I was to do that. It would accomplish nothing for me to attempt to justify myself. That would not be considered acceptable. So I went to the woman and told her that I was sorry for making such an insinuative and insensitive remark and asked for her forgiveness. My apology was accepted. No longer would her feelings of hurt limit her to the bench. No longer would my feelings of pride in the matter bench me, causing my ministry to her to be ineffective.

Pride and self-will are tightly integrated traits that work to prevent meaningful relationships. They are the breeding ground for selfishness and disregard for others. While some members of society honor the macho image, God does not. In fact, He tells us in His Word that He hates it. Pride ministers to self-serving interests. It is destructive.

There was a time in my life when I was confined for several months in a low security camp for an environmental charge that was brought against a company I owned. During that time, I sought out Christian inmates for fellowship. Soon I was singing in a men's chorus and teaching a Bible Study class. But no one could play the piano at the Chapel services, so all of the singing was *a capella*.

One day, I was pleasantly surprised to see a new inmate attend the Sunday morning service. His name was Tom. He asked if he could sing and play a special song. We were delighted to give him audience. The song he sang was *El Shaddai*, a song sung by Amy Grant. The following Sunday he asked me to sing a duet with him. I did. His piano accompaniment was beautiful.

But Tom had some problems. He took pride in his macho image. You know. Nobody is going to push me around and get away with it. Very self-assertive and vocal. And I was appalled at his language. Speech of the streets. Dirty. Distorted with sexual references to illicit acts. Not becoming of a follower of Christ.

Several weeks later I was hurt and shocked to hear that Tom had picked a fight with Fred, a friend of mine, and both of them had been transferred to other places without an opportunity for me to say good-bye.

I liked Fred. He was amiable and conscientious. He lived near Block Island, New York, and knowing my interest in travel and remote scenic places, he described Block Island to me in vivid detail. The ferry boat ride. The old lighthouse. Cliffs and beaches. The night before his forced departure we had walked several miles together around the compound in deep discussion. He had served about seven years of a ten year sentence. Time was taking a heavy toll on his family. As we parted, he told me our talk was the most meaningful conversation he had with anyone since his confinement.

But in a few more hours havoc struck. Tom had been assigned work detail with the construction crew. He was working on a job with Fred. Fred had seniority. He was the truck driver for the work crew. But Tom demanded to drive and words were exchanged. Suddenly Tom threw a punch to Fred's eye. Fred retaliated. The fight was soon stopped, but relationships were broken.

That's the way pride is. It creates barriers and alienates. It benches. It causes our testimony and work for Christ to become ineffective.

***B**UT IF YOU HAVE BITTER
ENVY AND SELF-SEEKING
IN YOUR HEARTS,
DO NOT BOAST AND LIE
AGAINST THE TRUTH.
FOR WHERE ENVY AND
SELF-SEEKING EXIST,
CONFUSION AND EVERY
EVIL THING ARE THERE.
JAMES 3:14, 16.*

Frank H Leaman

Envy and Jealousy

Envy sounds like a little word. Not so bad. Sometimes envy can even help to motivate us to do better. Encourage us to try harder. Are we sure of that?

We only need to consider that it was envy that caused the Pharisees to demand Jesus' crucifixion to recognize the terrible evil power envy can deliver. Its blow has caused the fall of kingdoms. It creates rifts that place canyons between people. It is capable of releasing rivers of blood.

It is shamefully common to find envy and strife disrupting the fellowship of God's people.

> Long standing feuds.
> Breakdown of communication.
> Members who refuse to associate with one another.
> Criticism, slander and gossip.

Churches often criticize other churches and enter into destructive competition. Even pastors can become jealous of other pastors.

Jesus' disciples were no different. They also were a feuding bunch who had conflicts soaked in envy. The mother of James and John petitioned Jesus that her sons would be granted the privilege to sit one on His right hand and one on His left in His coming kingdom. When the other disciples heard it, they became very indignant. They reasoned that they should have positions of honor also.

Jesus replied, "Whosoever will be chief among you, let him be your servant." Matthew 20:27.

We need to see Jesus again and again, the Alpha and the Omega, the King of Kings and Lord of Lords, bending His knees and washing the disciples' dirty feet.

From the Bible stories we heard as children about the Philistines, we view them as a warring people who frequently fought against the Israelites. But they were not always like this. At one time they were a righteous nation. In fact, there was a time when Abraham sojourned in the land of the Philistines with his flocks and herds because there was a famine in the land of Canaan. From what we are told about Abimilech, King of the Philistines, he was an upright man who worshipped Jehovah as Abraham did. The Lord said of him, "I know the integrity of your heart." Genesis 20:6.

Abimilech entreated Abraham kindly, granted him permission to graze his cattle anywhere he pleased in his country and even gave him gifts.

Years later, Abimilech offered the same grace to Isaac when another famine spread across the land of Canaan. He even encouraged Isaac to plant crops in his country and reap harvests. God richly blessed Isaac. His harvests became very great.

Then other seeds were sown. Not in soil. In hearts. Not good seeds. Bad seeds. As Isaac's possessions increased, the Philistines began to envy him. Finally, the situation got so out of control that Abimilech had to ask Isaac to leave his country.

But the seeds of envy continued to grow. More minerals for seeds. More water. Arrows. Border raids. Full scale invasions. More wars. More blood. Until the prophet Zephaniah prophesied against the Philistines with the word of the Lord saying, "I will destroy you so there shall be no inhabitant." Zephaniah 2:5. Today in our world there are no Philistines. Not only were they benched, they were annihilated. Envy choked away their very existence.

When David slew the giant, Goliath, the Israelites praised him greatly. Saul, who was the King of Israel, soon heard women singing in the streets of Jerusalem, "Saul has slain his thousands, and David his ten thousands." I Samuel 18:7.

King Saul became enraged with jealousy. He attempted to kill David with a javelin, but David escaped. For several years, Saul sought David like a bloodhound with three thousand chosen men, even when he knew that the Lord was with David and had anointed David to be the next King for His people. When David was aided by Ahimelech, the Priest, Saul ordered the execution of Ahimelech and his household and the people of his city. So great was his rage and his rebellion against God. He was caught in a whirlpool of jealousy and self-destruction that ultimately took his life.

For many years, Joab was the captain of King David's army. Usually, he faithfully fulfilled the wishes of his king, but one time he directly and willfully disobeyed the king's command. Absalom, one of David's sons, stormed Jerusalem in a thundering raid to take over the throne, and David and his servants were forced to flee. During the next several days a significant number of people who were loyal to

David came to his aid. When a battle was fought several days later in the woods of Ephraim between those loyal to David and those who had aligned themselves with Absalom, David gave Joab and those who bore the sword for him explicit instruction not to harm Absalom, but to capture him alive. However, in the battle, Joab came upon Absalom, who was hanging by his hair from the boughs of a large oak tree and threw three darts into Absalom's heart. According to Joab the penalty for treason was death, even though King David had chosen to show mercy.

Because of Joab's disobedience, David relieved him of his duties and made Amasa the captain of his host. Joab became angry and jealous. Soon he found an occasion to eliminate his rival. He came upon Amasa while he was unarmed on the highway at Gibeon and struck him with his sword, killing him.

Jealousy can muster a terrible driving force that births irrational behavior. When acted out to satisfy some neurotic need the result is always harmful. Often disastrous.

Leo Buscaglia in his book *Loving Each Other* states, "We are responsible for our jealousy, no one else. Blaming others for what we feel, can lead nowhere. Change will only begin when we are willing to accept our jealousy as our responsibility. Persons who cling to jealousy destroy themselves." He mentions some different ways we handle our jealousy.

> Aggression - fight for what we believe is rightfully ours.
> Rationalization - tell ourselves that the other person is inferior to us.
> Repression - attempt to bury our feelings.
> Withdrawal - escape the situation by convincing ourselves that what we don't know can't hurt us.
> Playing the martyr - suffer in silence and do nothing about it.
> Playing the sadist - seek ways to hurt and get even.
> Recognizing jealousy as a warning of "something wrong" - a positive step to its being corrected.

As the people of God, we would do well to saturate our beings with the admonition of the Apostle Paul.

"Fill up and complete my joy by living in harmony and being of the same mind and in purpose, having the same love, being in full accord and of one harmonious mind and intention. Do nothing from factional motives through contentiousness, strife, selfishness or for unworthy ends, or prompted conceit and empty arrogance. Instead, in a true spirit of humility let each regard others as better than and superior to himself thinking more highly of one another than you do of yourselves. Let each esteem and look upon and be concerned for not merely his own interest, but also each for the interest of others." Philippians 2:2-4, TAB.

Again quoting Leo Buscaglia, "Jealousy diminishes only when we regain a feeling of worth and self-respect, stop internalizing the problem and begin to view it objectively as something stemming from our personal demands and needs. The essential decision is whether we will allow our jealousy to become an all-consuming monster, capable of destroying us and those we love, or become a challenge for us to grow in self-respect and personal knowledge."

Envy and jealousy need not glue us to the bench and imprison us. As we discover anew the marvelous grace of God and open our hearts to receive it, we will find sufficient grace to retire these evil feelings that bind us. We will again become free to participate effectively in the game.

*I HAVE GONE ASTRAY
LIKE A LOST SHEEP;
SEEK YOUR SERVANT;
FOR I DO NOT FORGET
YOUR COMMANDMENTS.
PS. 119:176.*

Losing One's Way

There are times when God's people simply wander away from the action God has called them to and they find themselves on the bench, a place where happiness becomes transient and long term satisfaction from living is denied. The thrill of conquest and victory is no longer their experience.

The *Parable of the Sower*, Matthew 13, and the story of the *Good Shepherd*, Matthew 18, shed some light on how this happens. In the first parable, Jesus told the story of a sower who scattered seed. Some seed fell into thorny soil. It germinated and brought forth life, but in time the thorns crowded around it and choked the plants of value. Jesus interpreted the meaning of this to His disciples by explaining that the thorns represented the cares of this world and the deceitfulness of riches. The pursuit of materialism can choke us and make us unfruitful. We become distracted and lose our way. We yield to the temptation of pursuing our interests rather than God's purposes for us. We attempt to solve the cares and demands that living deals out to us without looking to God for help. Living becomes lonely, shallow and without purpose.

The late John Paul Getty, at one time known as one of the world's richest men, once said, "I would give all that I have to find inner peace." Riches can make us comfortable, but they cannot fill our hearts with joy and peace.

A chaplain who works for the Bureau of Prisons told me he thought early in his life that education was his ticket to happiness. His drive to become educated enabled him to achieve two Bachelor's degrees, a Master's degree and finally a Doctorate degree. But, upon attaining his goal, he found that he was still the same person with the same dissatisfaction. He felt empty. Unfulfilled. Unhappy. And he didn't understand why.

Then his life was suddenly changed by an accident that was very nearly fatal. Through the struggle of recovery, he found the Lord as his personal Savior. He became transformed. The knowledge that he had in his head about Christ became real in his heart. His life was changed. In answer to God's call, he became a minister of the gospel.

Isaiah the prophet wrote, "All we like sheep have gone astray. We have turned everyone to his own way." Isaiah 53:6. Sheep can only see about fifteen feet in front of them. They become lost easily. They are very dependent on their shepherd. The wonder of the story of the Good Shepherd is not that a sheep went astray from the flock and found itself in peril. It is the depth of the Shepherd's love as he went out into the darkness to save the sheep from a certain death.

John tells us in his Gospel that at one time Jesus had many disciples, but there came a time when many of his disciples walked no more with Him. John 6:66. They had lost their way. Instead of following Jesus, they began to value other things as more important. Their eyes were attracted to illusions of better things with which to fill their time. They expended their energy in pursuing other interests. In doing so, they traded life in the kingdom of God where nothing is lost, to life in this world where everything is ultimately lost.

Those of us who would be servants of our Lord dare not lose our sense of His mission and purpose for us. We are called to consistent obedience and faithfulness. There are times when our desires and goals must be placed aside to answer His call to us. There are times when the way He leads becomes difficult for us. He hasn't promised us an easy road as we follow Him, but He has promised us unspeakable joy and newness of life. The disciples of Jesus who remained faithful and witnessed their Lord's resurrected presence were soon turning the world upside down telling the Gospel message. While others were benched, they were blessed with power. They were filled with joy!

Almost four thousand years ago, a man named Lot, Abraham's nephew, began to wander away from the will of God. Genesis 13. Lot was blessed in abundance with flocks and herds and servants as he sojourned throughout the land of Canaan with Abraham. There came a time, however, when strife arose between Lot's herdsmen and Abraham's herdsmen. Because of the tremendous size of their herds of cattle and flocks of sheep, grazing became difficult. Finally, Abraham told Lot that it was necessary for them to separate their flocks and herds to avoid further strife. Being a man of peace, Abraham gave Lot first choice for grazing country. Lot chose the plain of Jordan because it was well watered.

Soon Lot began to wander away from God's desires for him. He pitched his tent toward Sodom. That may not seem significant, but it represented a change in direction. Sodom was known for its wickedness and acts of violence and abuse. In time, Lot found a market place in Sodom and he sold his flocks and herds. Then he accepted the position of judge in Sodom and sat at the gate of the city to settle disputes. Meanwhile, his servants and his family became engulfed in the evil around them. Soon their desire to obey and serve Jehovah was overrun with worldly concerns and wickedness.

When the Lord revealed to Abraham by angelic visitors that the people of Sodom were going to be destroyed because of their evil deeds, Abraham interceded for Lot and his family. Genesis 18. Sodom was not spared from destruction, but an angel was dispatched to offer escape for Lot and his family. Lot's sons-in-law refused to leave. While Lot, his wife and daughters fled across the plain, Lot's wife disobeyed God's command not to look back toward Sodom. She left Sodom as the angel bade her, but Sodom was still in her heart. She was possessed by what she had left behind. Her home. Her earthly treasures. As she glanced backward, she became a pillar of salt. Lot lost his wife. He lost all his wealth and all of his servants. Benching is not only a loss to God, it is a loss to God's people.

We cannot wander away from our Lord without suffering loss. The bench becomes hard and painful. Yet God in His mercy seeks us there and provides opportunity for escape. He wants us back in the game. Gently He leads us back to a place of usefulness and service. He once again places us in a position of blessing.

I had a great Sunday School teacher during my early teenage years. Bill taught the boys class. He took a keen interest in us. Since our church didn't have a program for youth, occasionally he would take us hiking and backpacking. I still have fond memories of the exciting experiences we had together on the trails, in lean-tos and around camp fires. I remember some of the tales he used to tell us that were intended to keep us from leaving our sleeping bags during the night.

There came a time, however, soon after Bill married, when ambitions to get ahead financially began to take away time to serve in the church. He ceased teaching. Then, he and his wife had a daughter. That took more time. They bought a new home. Furniture was needed. Then they purchased a new car. His work week became more and more intense. In time, church attendance ceased. Doing the Lord's work was replaced with a goal to become independently wealthy. This process occurred subtly over a period of several years. In effect, Bill had wandered away and found himself on the bench.

Persons in our church began praying for him. I remember his name being mentioned many times in the Wednesday night prayer services. Then, the economy took a downward turn. Bill became unemployed. This difficulty brought him to the realization that he had moved from a position of joy to misery. He rededicated his life to the Lord, and followed the Lord's leading to attend Lancaster School of the Bible. After graduation, he and his family became missionaries in the island of Grenada. We rejoiced! It was wonderful to witness his moving from the bench to the mission field. Joy is in the cup of service. This joy became his.

When I was twelve years old, there was a man in my church who I believed was a dedicated servant of the Lord. He held street meetings in a slum area of our city that was later razed and converted into apartment buildings. Following my baptism, he gave me an invitation to attend a street meeting. I went.

Our small group gathered together at a street corner and began to sing songs of the faith. A considerable number of children and adults soon gathered around. Some brought dilapidated chairs to sit on. Older adults came outside and sat on their house steps. The poverty of these people struck me. It made me feel ashamed that they were so poor and had hopelessness etched into their faces, while others nearby were blessed with so much and apparently weren't helping them. I wondered if our church could do more than just have a meeting on the street for them.

As my little mind was churning these thoughts over, suddenly the man who had invited me to come asked me in front of everybody to give my testimony. For several seconds, I was completely paralyzed. I had heard people give testimonies in my church, but I had never given one or even thought about giving one. In my panic, I could only breath a brief prayer to Jesus, asking Him to help me like He helped His disciples. Nervously, I stepped forward to the spot the man was indicating for me to stand. What happened next I will never forget. Within moments a power charged through my body that drove out all fear. I began to speak of Jesus and share about His love for me and my love for Him. A testimony of several minutes duration poured from my lips. It was a direct instant anointing of the Holy Spirit.

It would have been great if my memory of the leader of our group that day could have remained untainted. But as time passed, I watched him fall. He was a large tomato farmer. As a youth, I worked in his fields picking tomatoes for ten cents a basket. One year misfortune struck. He lost the market for his ripened tomatoes. They rotted in the fields.

Out of necessity, he found employment with a trucking firm and began long distance driving. His new occupation not only removed him from involvement in the church, it exposed him full force to the world of faith mockers, blasphemers, alcoholics and prostitutes. A mission field of endless opportunities. But he, like Lot of old, pitched his tent toward Sodom. A little yielding to temptation. Just a little. Then a little more. And yet more. Until he became bound by the forces of evil and lost his desire to live for Christ.

A gradual process. A fog moving in that blinded spiritual vision and resulted in losing the way. It takes clear vision to stay on the straight and narrow way that leads to eternal life. We are instructed to "walk in the light." I John 1:7.

It is so easy for us to make provision for a little sin. To turn our tents in another direction just a little bit. But little sins have a way of growing. The Apostle Peter wrote a stern warning for these who turn from the Saviour and allow themselves to be overcome by evil.

> "For if after they have escaped the pollutions of the world through the knowledge of the Lord and Saviour Jesus Christ, they are again entangled therein, and overcome, the latter end is worse with them than the beginning. For it had been better for them not to have known the way of righteousness, then, after they have known it, to turn from the holy commandment delivered unto them." II Peter 2:20,21.

Nothing is as eternally fatal as a fall from the bench. Peering toward the deceptive pool of evil screened with bright lights and a masquerade of pleasure invites a fall into the abyss of damnation.

We can easily become lost in the crowd that worships materialism, pursues the glamour of sin and disregards God. We can even become lost in the church. Luke chapter fifteen gives us much insight into the condition of the lost and the will of God to seek the lost. The chapter opens with a large crowd of publicans and sinners gathering around Jesus. Around the perimeter of this crowd of street scum, pious Pharisees and scribes positioned themselves with critical ears tuned into Jesus' frequency. And Jesus, recognizing that His entire audience was lost, began to tell them some stories about lost things and lost persons.

He told them about a sheep that became lost unknowingly. It didn't want to be lost, but it carelessly strayed from the flock. Fear gripped the sheep when it realized that it was beyond the shepherd's voice. It wandered about in panic as night fell. It began to bleat, sounding a cry for help.

Later, while securing his flock in the fold, the shepherd realized that one of the sheep was missing. He went out into the night, retracing his steps, listening to hear the sound of his bleating sheep. During his searching, he heard the cry of his sheep and followed the sound until he had found it. Then he returned home rejoicing because he had found the sheep that was lost.

The sheep in this story depicts persons who know that they are lost and cry out to God for help. God's ears are always ready to hear and He comes speedily to give His salvation.

Jesus continued His storytelling. He told the crowd about a woman who owned ten pieces of silver. When she realized that one of the silver pieces was missing, she searched and swept her house diligently until she found it. Then she rejoiced greatly.

The coin was lost unknowingly and indifferently. It couldn't have cared if it ever was found or not. But the owner of the coin cared greatly that the coin be found.

So everyone in the crowd who Jesus addressed that day, was lost in one way or another. All were owned by the Creator. All were being sought by Him whether they cared to be found or whether they didn't. It is most enlightening to note that Jesus ended the story of the lost coin by saying, "There is joy in the presence of the angels of God over one sinner who repents." Luke 15:10. In this vivid statement, Jesus made clear the necessity of repentance for becoming found. He also emphasized the delight a repentant heart brings to Him.

Finally, Jesus told His diverse crowd the parable of the lost son. A young lad who prematurely without respect asked for his share of his father's estate in a culture where this act was an extreme insult. It meant that the son wished his father was dead so he could have his money. To have this happen was a severe disgrace. A time of bitter mourning that occasionally took fathers to early graves.

In the story, the son became lost willingly by choice, but he was ignorant of the consequences that would eventually press against him. His foolish life lead to emptiness, misery and hunger. In time his rebellious spirit was broken. He experienced a change of heart, prepared a sincere and humble confession and decided to return to his home. There his father was waiting. His father's eyes had been fixed on the path that lead home for many days. And when he recognized his son, his heart leaped with joy. He ran to meet his son and hugged and kissed him, not waiting for words of remorse and apology. It didn't matter that his son was skinny and filthy. His clothing and hair ragged and smelling like pigs. His son had returned! It was celebration time! A ring. A robe. New shoes. A fattened calf. A party. Music. Dancing.

But Jesus didn't end the story there. Pharisees and scribes were murmuring and jesting among themselves along the edges of the crowd. So Jesus included the likes of them in His story also. He told of an older son who had remained faithful to his father all his life, doing his father's bidding. As this son was returning from working in the fields, he questioned a servant concerning the occasion for the celebration he was hearing. When he learned that his brother had returned and the party was in his honor, he seethed in anger and refused to join in the festivity.

So the father left the party, seeking his oldest son who also was lost. A self-righteous son who didn't understand or appreciate the loving heart of his father. A son who didn't realize that he needed grace to the same degree that his wayward brother did. A son who thought he had earned his father's love and deserved special privilege and status. A son who failed to realize that a father's inheritance to any son is a gift that cannot be bought.

And here the story ends. Jesus didn't say if the oldest son repented and joined in the celebration for his brother or not. But one thing is certain. The heart of the oldest son was exposed in all its ugliness. Intolerant. Condemning. Proud. Envious. Ungrateful.

Unfortunately, the Pharisees and scribes would not concede that it was as difficult for the father to love his older son as his younger son. That both were equally unworthy of the father's love. In time, in a horrendous act driven by envy they had the very personification of God's love, the Incarnate Son of God, crucified. They could not rejoice in His life or His teachings. They were benched in a lostness they were unable to comprehend, even while their feet daily trod the temple floors.

So we lose our way and need to be found. We can obey and follow only when our Shepherd is in view. Jesus put it this way.

> "My sheep hear my voice, and I know them, and they follow me: And I give them eternal life; and they shall never perish, neither shall anyone snatch them out of my hand." John 10:27,28.

*WE HAVE RENOUNCED
THE HIDDEN THINGS
OF DISHONESTY,
NOT WALKING IN CRAFTINESS,
NOR HANDLING THE
WORK OF GOD DECEITFULLY;
BUT BY MANIFESTATION
OF THE TRUTH
COMMENDING OURSELVES
TO EVERY MAN'S CONSCIENCE
IN THE SIGHT OF GOD.
II COR. 4:2.*

Frank H Leaman

Dishonesty

Throughout the Bible, we, as the people of God, are admonished to be honest with God and with one another. By being dishonest, we misrepresent the character of our Heavenly Father who is holy. We place ourselves beyond the realm of His blessing.

We do not think of Abraham, the Father of God's people Israel, as having a problem with dishonesty. Yet, there was a time when his faith was weak and dishonesty got him into grave trouble. The Promised Land became stricken with a famine. Concerned about the welfare of his flocks and herds, he felt the fertile tributaries of the Nile beckoning him. He decided to journey to Egypt for relief. But in going, he traded one crisis for another. Genesis 12:10-20.

Abraham's wife, Sarah, also his half sister, was very beautiful. Abraham reasoned that if the Egyptians learned that Sarah was his wife, they would kill him and take her. He knew that the Pharaoh sought the most beautiful women for his harem. So he instructed Sarah to tell the Egyptians that she was his sister. In our way of thinking, we would tend to call this only a white lie since it was half truth. But the untruth brought severe consequences.

When the Egyptian princes saw how attractive Sarah was, they hastened to tell Pharaoh about the woman from Canaan that he should meet. Soon Sarah was taken into Pharaoh's house.

Abraham received gifts of oxen and camels and servants, but he didn't like the trade. What a predicament!

Then God came to Abraham's rescue. He caused a gruesome plague to fall upon Pharaoh and his house. Pharaoh sought a reason for the plague. He discovered that Sarah was actually Abraham's wife. He became extremely angry. In no uncertain terms he commanded Abraham and his wife to flee with their servants and possessions. Abraham was benched. He had lost an opportunity to witness for his God in Pharaoh's court.

Abraham knew the way back was through repentance. When he arrived in Canaan, he prepared an altar and called upon the Lord for forgiveness. Leaving the bench to get back in the game, he was once again free to serve his God.

Another of the patriarchs, Jacob, is remembered for being a deceiver because he tricked his brother Esau into trading his birthright for a bowl of porridge. His dishonesty brought Esau's wrath upon him, and he was forced to leave his home and flee to his uncle's place in Haran. Genesis 29-31. There he was benched for twenty years.

During this time in Haran, he was deceived and cheated by his uncle many times over. Often his wages were changed to his uncle's advantage. He was even tricked into marrying Laban's unattractive daughter, Leah, when he thought he was marrying her sister, Rachel. Again and again he learned what it felt like to be treated dishonestly. His schooling was difficult, but when he finally moved from the bench, he was a changed man. God noticed this and gave him a new name, Israel, meaning a prince of God.

Several hundred years later, when the children of Israel entered the Promised Land, they were given explicit instructions concerning the conquest of Jericho. The Lord had told his servant, Joshua, that all of the silver, gold and vessels of brass and iron found in the city were to be consecrated to God and placed in the Lord's treasury. The city and all other possessions in it were to be destroyed by fire. During the conquest, however, one of the Israelites, Achan, secretly took two hundred shekels of silver, a wedge of gold and a Babylonish garment and buried them in the ground beneath his tent. Joshua 7.

The next battle Israel fought was against a small town. During this battle involving over four thousand warriors, the Lord's blessing of victory was withheld. The army of Israel was forced to retreat, leaving their dead behind. In exasperation, Joshua asked the Lord why they were defeated. God replied that there was sin in the camp of Israel. All Israel was benched. They were no longer able to wage conquest successfully.

Joshua gathered the people together. He informed them that the Lord had told him that sin in the camp had caused the defeat. He asked for the guilty to come forward and confess. No one responded. Finally, lots were cast to determine who was guilty. Achan's tribe was selected. Still there was no confession. Lots were then cast to find out which family in the tribe was guilty. The lot fell on Achan's family. Again, no confession was made. Another lot was cast to discover which household was guilty. The lot fell on Achan's household. Only then did Achan confess his sin.

Messengers were dispatched to Achan's tent and the stolen goods were found. The penalty was severe. Achan and his family who had conspired to keep his secret were slain with stones. The sin was eradicated. The camp was cleansed. Israel could again be victorious.

It is clear from these examples in the Bible that dishonesty is a sin that God will not tolerate in His people. As the children of God, we can be certain that He will not overlook dishonesty in us either.

Some years ago, I managed an engineering group for a large connector company that had numerous manufacturing facilities in several states. A brilliant engineer on my staff was regarded as a fine Christian and was well liked. He had considerable potential for advancement. One day, he told me that he was planning to take his family to the beach for a vacation. I realized that on the way he would be passing one of the plants in Virginia where my Department had responsibility for a project. I explained to him that if he would be willing to spend two hours at that plant on his way, the company would pay for his travel expenses to and from the plant he would be visiting. He agreed to this assignment.

When he returned from his vacation, he filled out an expense voucher for approval and payment. During the approval process, a call was made to the Plant Manager at the Virginia plant. It was learned that the engineer had not signed the plant's visitor's log. The receptionist would not have permitted entrance into the plant without obtaining a signature.

The engineer was then confronted with the conflicting evidence. He knew of a side entrance to the building and hastened to explain that he had used that entrance instead of the front entrance. Another call was made to the Virginia plant. The Plant Manager reported that the side entrance had been out of use for over a month due to a building modification.

When the engineer was told about the side entrance, he had to admit that he was lying. He explained that his family was delayed in leaving their home, so he didn't stop at the plant. He attempted to cover his assigned responsibility by making a telephone call.

The news of his dishonesty caused an already approved salary increase to be withdrawn. Within a month, the engineer left the company for employment elsewhere. His reputation had been dealt a serious blow. He had placed himself on a bench of ineffectiveness.

When I was six years old, I received an unforgettable lesson on the consequences of dishonesty. While shopping with my mother in a Christian bookstore, I became captivated by the many little toys, pencils and books all around me. Beautiful crosses and pictures of Jesus. This entire store was a new experience for me. I was bubbling with excitement. While my mother was being assisted by the store clerk, I went wandering. As my little eyes were scanning the contents of shelves and counters, suddenly I spotted some small booklets that had very shiny pages. One page was the prettiest gold I had ever seen. Other pages were green, red, white and black. The moment I saw them I wanted some.

Having a mother who I thought said "no" too many times when I wanted something, I pondered in my mind what I would do. I wanted those books so badly. When I looked toward my mother and the clerk, their backs were turned toward me. In an instant, I grabbed one of the books and put it in my pocket. It fit in my pocket so nicely and taking it was so easy. Another glance at their backs. Another grab for more books. Five. That should be enough. Suddenly, I knew I had done wrong. The spot I was standing on became very uncomfortable. Almost threatening. I moved away quickly and continued my wandering. More glances confirmed that I had not been seen.

But then I remembered another time when I had sneaked a forbidden cookie from a kitchen table top. I had carefully and quietly concealed myself under the table out of view, then sneaked a hand over the table edge and took a cookie. So smart. So simple. So cool. But, while I was still chewing the first bite, my mother said, "God saw you take that cookie."

"No, He didn't!" I exclaimed emphatically. "I'm under the table and He can't see me!"

"Oh yes, He can see you," my mother had insisted. "He can see right through table tops, roofs, anything. God always sees everything that we do."

I knew God had seen me take those pretty books. I didn't feel good thinking about that. But, somehow I was able to mask my guilt sufficiently to get by without being questioned.

Once home, I was certain that there would be trouble if the books were ever found. So I went to the attic and slipped them into a cupboard drawer.

Months passed and I had almost forgotten about the books when exposure time arrived. Our family was entertaining friends. We children went to the attic to play. The eye-catching books were discovered by a little girl. Before I could stop her, she bounded down two flights of stairs, ran into the living room and exclaimed to her mother, "Mommy, I want some pretty books like these too."

Heads turned and eyes rolled as my mother turned to me and asked, "Frank, where did you get these books?"

I couldn't answer. A lump formed in my throat that kept me speechless. Pay day. I turned and ran upstairs to my room. Followed? Of course. And drilled to a full confession. I was thinking I was about to get my worst punishment ever. But no. I was getting off easy. No spanking. My Mother told me, "The man who owns the store where you stole those books is speaking at our church on Sunday and he is coming to our home for dinner. You will need to tell him what you did and give the books back to him."

"Wow! I was lucky," I thought, and soon forgot about my assignment.

But Sunday morning I remembered. Did I ever squirm in church! Once home, my mother told me that I was to go to the man with the stolen goods when the adults retired to the living room right after dinner. I was so nervous and frightened that I couldn't eat. Even chocolate cake didn't taste good. I asked to be excused and fled to my bedroom.

When the kitchen duties were finished, my mother came to my room, placed the books in my hand and told me, "Frank, now it is time to tell the man what you did."

A very reluctant step encouraged by threat of a hard spanking if I didn't. Then another. It seemed like it took fifteen minutes to get to the living room. Maybe more. Steps were never so hard or so slow for me than that day. By the time I reached the living room, I was crying.

But, soon I found myself on the knee of a gentle man who accepted the books and assured me of his forgiveness. I was also instructed about the importance of asking God for His forgiveness. Then it was all over. I was again free to get on with my life. So it seemed at the time. Yet, in a sense even now, I don't feel that this experience, this lesson, is totally over. I have never been able to forget it.

It is important that we learn early in life that dishonesty has the power to bring disharmony between our spirits and the Spirit of God. We cannot effectively perform the tasks God gives us when caught in webs of dishonesty. Ultimately, we will find ourselves benched and out of the game.

BUT WITHOUT FAITH
IT IS IMPOSSIBLE
TO PLEASE HIM:
FOR HE WHO COMES TO GOD
MUST BELIEVE THAT HE IS,
AND THAT HE IS A
REWARDER OF THOSE
WHO DILIGENTLY SEEK HIM.
HEBREWS 11:6.

Frank H Leaman

Doubting God

There is a direct correlation between the way we view God and what we believe He is able to perform. If God is a mere object to us, a philosophy of life or a subject of mythology, such a god can do nothing beyond our own capabilities. If, on the other hand, we see Him as the Almighty One, the Creator of the heavens and the earth, His power to do is without limit.

Some believe in the God of the Bible and others do not. Even among those who believe in God, there are those who believe with the head and those who believe with the heart. To believe with the heart is to surrender one's self to God's purposes and obey His commands. This results in worship and service. The world cannot deny that believing in God with the heart makes a difference in the way we live.

A number of years ago I attended a technical conference in San Francisco. I arrived at the hotel early in the evening, changed into casual clothing and went to the lobby to peruse the hotel restaurant's menus. I noticed how expensive the dinners were and reasoned that I could find something cheaper elsewhere to satisfy my hunger. I left the hotel and began walking down the street. Within a few moments a girl began walking close beside me. I heard her saying, "Take me to your room and I'll take you to paradise."

I stopped and looked at her. She was young and very pretty. Her dress was scant and sexy. Her eyes were inviting an affirmative answer.

I replied, "I don't know if you have ever read the Bible, but in the Book of Proverbs, chapter seven, men are strongly advised not to do what you are suggesting. I believe the Bible is the Word of God and I do my best to live by it."

She retorted, "Well, I don't believe a word of it." She spun around and headed in the other direction like I was inflicted with some terrible plague.

I had to ponder her remark. Yes, there was a difference between us. She didn't believe in the God of the Bible and I did. To her, sin against God was without consequence. To me, disobeying the commands of God invited God's judgment.

But even when we have a strong belief in the God of the Bible, times of trauma can force our faith into obscurity. We become

107

haunted by questions that seem unanswerable. Doubt begins to crawl across our souls. It works to extinguish our view of God's capabilities and His interest in us. Soon we find ourselves doubting God's presence. In our belief system, truth subtly changes to untruth. We reason that God doesn't care. That people don't care. Sometimes despair catches up with us to the extent that *we* no longer care. Ironically, we withdraw into a shell of isolationism just when we need others and God the most.

John the Baptist had his preaching ministry brutally shut down by King Herod. John was thrown into prison. As the days passed, he began to doubt God's purposes. He wondered why he was suffering when he had so faithfully obeyed the call God had given him to proclaim the Word of the Lord. Living and sleeping in the desert. Eating locust and wild honey. Preaching a message of repentance until his voice became hoarse. He wondered if Jesus, the one he had baptized in the Jordan River when the voice of God spoke from heaven, really was the Messiah. Clouds of doubt began to confuse his mind. He finally dispatched his disciples to ask Jesus if He indeed was the Messiah, the Promised One of Israel.

Jesus replied, "Go tell John about what you see and hear. The blind receive their sight, the lame walk, the lepers are cleansed, the deaf hear, the dead are raised up, and the poor have the gospel preached to them. Blessed is he who is not offended by me." Luke 7:22. In His reply He was quoting prophecy from Isaiah that He knew John would recognize. Then He turned to the multitude and said, "John was more than a prophet. He was the messenger before my face to prepare the way before me. Among them that are born of women there has not risen a greater, than John the Baptist."

I can hear John the Baptist, upon receiving the message from his disciples, saying "Yes. Indeed. He is the Promised One," as he pressed against the bars that constrained him.

Doubting God robs us of blessing. This truth is powerfully evident in the record we have of Jesus' ministry. He had traveled to Capernaum, to the country of the Gergesenes, throughout the cities and towns of Galilee and along the shores of the Sea of Tiberias teaching and healing the sick. Great multitudes followed Him. But when He returned home to Nazareth, He could not perform mighty works of healing there because of their unbelief. In Nazareth, the people viewed Jesus as Joseph's son. Some charged that He was an illegitimate child. The religious leaders retorted, "What good can come out of Nazareth?" John 1:46.

Jesus always responded to faith in persons. It was their faith that placed them in the multitudes.

> People sought Him.
> People called out to Him.
> People stretched to touch Him.

And Jesus couldn't help but notice them. His compassion flowed. Sometimes He gave them instructions. "Go show yourselves to the priests." "Go wash your eyes and you will see." "Rise up and walk." But without faith, positive results could not happen. Lack of faith limited Jesus' power to save, to heal and to bless, even when He desired so much to share His love and grace with everyone.

Yes, it was Jesus, the tireless man from Nazareth, who cried over the city of Jerusalem, "How often I would have gathered your children together as a hen gathers her brood under her wings, and you would not." Luke 13:34 RSV.

Faith is not stored away like money in the bank. Growing in faith is a constant process of daily renewing our trust in Jesus. In the Gospel of Mark, chapter 9, the disciples of Jesus were unable to cast out an evil spirit that had caused a boy to be epileptic and mute. This scene begins with a ruckus among the crowd. The teachers of the law were arguing with the disciples of Jesus. The Jewish religious leaders often attempted to put down the followers of Jesus and sway the crowds to their favor. No doubt their artful design was to convey their own philosophies and sentiments that Jesus was not the Messiah of Israel who had been promised. They were well adept at sowing seeds of doubt. And as the event unfolds, it becomes obvious that they were successful in injecting doubt into the very hearts of the disciples.

When the multitude saw Jesus coming down from the mountain, they left the scribes and ran to meet Him. Jesus turned to the scribes and asked what they were arguing with His disciples about. Knowing that the intent of their arguing was devious, they gave no answer. The silence was broken when a man fell at Jesus' feet and begged Him to heal his son who was possessed with a devil. His son was greatly afflicted and the evil spirit within him drove him to commit suicidal acts. The man told Jesus that he had asked the disciples to heal his son, but they weren't able to do it. The disciples had experienced power failure. Prior to this event, Jesus had given the disciples authority to use His power and His name to heal the sick and to cast out evil spirits, but on this occasion, they could not do what Jesus had charged them to do.

So Jesus took control of the situation. He began by saying, "O unbelieving generation. How long shall I put up with you?" He was indicating that they were slow to believe that he was the Messiah and to put their trust in Him. Then Jesus asked the disciples to bring the boy to Him. When the evil spirit saw Jesus through the eyes of the boy, it threw the boy to the ground and caused him to roll around and foam at the mouth. The boy's father pleaded, "If you can do anything, take pity on us and help us." Jesus returned a statement in kind and said, "If you can believe, everything is possible." Jesus demanded faith and confidence in His power to heal. Immediately the boy's father cried out, "I do believe! Help me to overcome my unbelief!" Jesus was attempting to emphasize that it was not this man's faith that gave Him the power to heal the boy. Jesus always had the power. But the man's faith would release the power for his son's healing. What the boy's father was praying - and what he said was a prayer - was for Jesus to help him to overcome his unbelief so that the defect of his faith would not stand in the way of the blessing he was seeking for his son.

Upon that confession, Jesus took action. He commanded the deaf and mute spirit to come out of the boy and never enter him again. The evil spirit shrieked, shook the boy violently, then came out, leaving the boy in a state that appeared like death. Jesus took the boy by the hand and lifted him up.

End of story? Not quite. The disciples of Jesus still had a lesson to learn about faith. And they knew that. Later when the crowd had dispersed, they went inside a house to refresh themselves. At such times, Jesus limited His public ministry in order to train His disciples. It takes time to learn. Deep spiritual growth isn't instant, regardless of the quality of experience or teaching. So the disciples were about to learn more from the Master. Their big question was, "Why couldn't we cast out the evil spirit?" Jesus told them that it was because of their unbelief that they had not been able to do that. They lacked the faith in Christ which was necessary and doubted that they could be used of God to cure the boy, and therefore they could not. The scribes had temporarily planted seeds of doubt in their minds regarding who Jesus really was. The fact remained that Jesus required faith in those who would be the instruments to bring His power of deliverance from sin, infirmities and evil spirits to those in need.

Matthew, in his Gospel, continues this account with Jesus telling the disciples that if they had faith like a grain of mustard seed, they could remove mountains and nothing would be impossible to them. There is a principle of growth in the grain of the seed stretching forward to great results. Of all the herbs, the mustard seed is the smallest, yet it grows to become the largest. This is the picture Jesus used to illustrate faith. Jesus added that such faith could only be birthed by prayer and fasting. Undertakings that appear too difficult to accomplish, can happen by the work of faith. This degree of faith is kept vigorous only by much prayer - prayer that is given priority even above taking food for the body.

Even after the resurrection of Jesus, His disciples had difficulty believing God's intentions in the death and resurrection of the promised Messiah. When Jesus was crucified, the world disintegrated around Thomas. In his grief and pain, everything lost meaning. Hope vanished. The Lord he had trusted to establish a kingdom had been condemned by an angry mob and slain. He withdrew into a sea of skepticism. How could it all end this way? Why didn't the God of Heaven save his Master from death? Wasn't Jesus the Son of God? Without his Lord, how was he ever going to get his life back together?

When the wonderful news that Jesus was alive reached his deafened ears and traversed to his grief stricken heart, with tortured mind he responded, "Unless I see the nail marks in his hands and put my finger where the nails were, and put my hand into his side, I will not believe it."

At least he was honest in expressing his doubts. The events surrounding Jesus' death and burial seemed too final to him.

But Jesus returned to His disciples one week later and showed Himself especially to Thomas. With the door bolted and the windows barred, Jesus suddenly appeared in their midst. He turned toward Thomas and extended His hands, palms upward and said, "See my hands and put your finger in the nail prints." Then He pulled away His garment from His side and continued, "Reach out your hand and put it into my side. Stop doubting and believe." John 20:27.

Thomas was shaken to the core of his being. Miraculously, the evidence he had asked for stood before him. His burden of doubt left him like a freight train barreling down a mountain side. He fell before his living Lord and exclaimed, "My Lord and my God!"

Dare we say, "Show me, then I will believe?" Can any more evidence be gathered beyond what has already been presented? Can we learn to believe without seeing?

Jesus said to Thomas, "Blessed are those who have not seen me, and yet believed." Such belief is the very platter of salvation.

In the Garden of Eden the subtle attack of Satan was charged with the pointed question, "Did God say?" Genesis 3:1.

Sin had its birth on Earth as the powers of evil planted seeds of doubt in the minds of the world's first human couple. And even today, Satan still seals his victory and secures his footing in our lives by persuading us to doubt God's words and God's promises.

Just as doubt on that fateful day doused God's perfect creation in catastrophic tragedy, doubt today has the power to ruthlessly upset our lives and fling us into impoverishment.

We do have times when circumstances create clouds of doubt that restrict our vision and force us to the bench. These times of crisis defy explanation. We do not endure them by choice. But even in the midst of them, seeking the face of God turns suffering into glorious beauty and songs of praise.

Faith grows in a believing heart. My mother had a faith like that - a faith tried by storms. During my parents' third year as missionaries in Africa, my younger brother became critically ill with anemic dysentery. At the age of four months he dropped below his birth weight. After many days of not being able to keep food in his stomach, he finally became too weak to swallow. For several days, he lay near death in the mission hospital.

One afternoon, the British doctor told my mother that he was certain my brother would not live through the night. In uncontrollable tears, she walked the mile and a half path that led to the shore of Lake Victoria. There she pleaded with the Lord in earnest prevailing prayer to save my brother's life She finally prayed, "Lord, if you see that my child can bring you glory, save his life."

Upon praying this, although she didn't hear an audible voice, she sensed within her being that the Lord was telling her that my brother would live, and in three days she would take him home. With thanksgiving and elation in her heart, she ran back to the clinic praising God and told the doctor what the Lord had promised her. He thought that she was suffering from too many sleepless nights and had become mentally disturbed. He gave her a sedative and sent her home to get some rest.

The nurse, however, had overheard what my mother had said. Formula had not even been prepared that day because my brother had been too weak to take any the day before. The nurse prepared some formula and attempted to spoon feed my brother one last time. To her amazement, he took some and swallowed it. An even greater wonder was that the formula stayed down. By the following day, he was strong enough to take milk from a bottle. His diarrhea abated. His recovery was so remarkable that in three days my parents were able to bring him home and care for him there.

My mother had prayed for my brother's healing all along. Some logical questions would be, "Why wasn't he healed before he was so near death? Was the delay a test of faith? Was God setting the stage to maximize the glory that He would receive from the healing? Was the ultimate purpose to strengthen the faith of others? Would my brother's life have been spared without my mother's prevailing prayer at that critical time when he was hovering between life and death?" Only God knows. One thing we do know. This brother of mine is very active in a teaching and helping ministry. God is being glorified through his sacrificial living for Christ.

The faith journey for all believers in Jesus begins at the Cross. And along the way, our faith should be growing. The environment for seeds of faith to grow comprises recognition of needs that we cannot meet by our own efforts, a willingness to hear what God is saying to us, an eagerness to learn how to mature in our Christian lives, and hearts that stretch to believe what God is saying to us. We all need hearts like that. And by God's grace we can have hearts like that. Hearts that birth answers to our prayers, even miracles.

Several years later, this same brother developed a serious rupture. Because of the illness he had as an infant, his body remained frail. Yet he desperately tried to compete with others his age and he suffered the consequences. At our family physician's insistence, my brother was scheduled for surgery.

The following Sunday afternoon, my family went to visit my grandparents. They invited us to stay for dinner. There was a revival meeting in progress in a tent nearby where Little David, a sixteen year old, was preaching. My grandfather invited us to go with him to the service. My grandmother wasn't feeling well, so my mother stayed at the house with her.

The service was rather low key and orderly and the sermon was remarkably good for a teenage preacher. Following his sermon, Little David gave an invitation for persons to accept Jesus as their Savior from sin. Then he extended an invitation for any who were ill or had infirmities who desired prayer to come forward. My father and grandfather took my brother to the edge of the platform. Little David placed his hands on my brother's head and simply prayed, "Lord, heal this little boy," not even asking what his ailment was.

When we returned to my grandparent's home, my father told my mother what had happened. She examined my brother and confirmed that his rupture was completely gone. The bulge that had been present on his one side was no longer there. The next morning at the hospital, when the surgeon examined my brother, he stated to his surprise that there was no sign of the rupture and no surgery was necessary!

Few books that I have read struck my heartstrings and stirred my emotions as the book *Joni* did. In 1967, Joni Eareckson was paralyzed from the neck down in a diving accident. In her autobiography, an international best-seller, she reveals her struggle with anger, bitterness and doubt and tells about her desperate search for meaning, happiness and usefulness.

She shares with us, "Grief, remorse and depression swept over me like a thick, choking blanket. I wished and prayed I might die. My doubts began to be as deep-seated as my resentment. Who, or what is God? Certainly not a personal Being who cares for individuals. What's the use of believing when your prayers fall on deaf ears? Tell me how being in this condition for over a year 'works together for good.' What good? Where? When? My mind was a jumble of thoughts and philosophies. Logical, rational, intellectual positions were posed and just as quickly disposed of by opposing concepts, apparently just as valid. What was right? What was wrong? Truth? Oh, what a maze of confusion."

Her search finally led her back to the Bible. Her bitterness softened. She discovered that her purpose in life is to glorify God. Her sister Diana told her, "You don't have to know why God let you be hurt. The fact is, God knows - and that's all that counts. Just trust Him to work things out for good, eventually, if not right now. If God knows the ultimate purpose and meaning of things, then He can find, or give meaning to a paralyzed life, too. But you can't fight Him on it."

Later, Joni herself reasoned, "There has to be a personal God. He may choose not to reveal Himself to me in some spectacular way - but then, why should He? Was I any more important than the next person who had to find God and purpose by faith, not sight? Why should I be different?"

She rounded a corner in her experience with pain, left the bench behind and proceeded down Victory Lane. Soon she was creating drawings with pen in mouth and signing them "PTL" for "Praise The Lord". Her wheel chair became an instrument of joy in her life. She was mobile. She was free. Free to live. Free to tell. Young Life meetings. Youth for Christ rallies. Television appearances. The Today Show. Interviews with the Chicago Tribune and Sun-Times. I heard her in person give her testimony at a Billy Graham Crusade. Thank-you, God, for Joni!

God is faithful in hearing us. Nothing that strikes us can match His power or block His grace. He is Awesome! He is Love! His promises are not to be doubted, but believed. And believing God keeps us in the game.

*"FOR MY THOUGHTS
ARE NOT YOUR THOUGHTS,
NOR ARE YOUR WAYS
MY WAYS", SAYS THE LORD.
FOR AS THE HEAVENS ARE
HIGHER THAN THE EARTH,
SO ARE MY WAYS
HIGHER THAN YOUR WAYS,
AND MY THOUGHTS
THAN YOUR THOUGHTS.
ISA. 55:8, 9.*

Frank H Leaman

Failure to Consult God First

How often we, as God's people, take sides on an issue or give our support to a person or a project without consulting God for direction in our choice. It is so easy for us to assume that our degree of knowledge is sufficient and our decision-making skills are so refined that we are able to choose the best in a given situation.

> Hasn't experience been our teacher?
> Haven't we learned to make practical and wise choices?
> Don't we have a real good feeling about our decision?

We so easily forget how radical our God reasons; that He knows the end from each beginning and has purposes in view that we see dimly at best. How much it behooves us to reflect on the revelation penned by the prophet Isaiah.

> "For my thoughts are not your thoughts, neither are your ways my ways, says the Lord. For as the heavens are higher than the earth, so are my ways higher than your ways, and my thoughts than your thoughts." Isaiah 55:8,9.

Rebekah, the beautiful bride of Isaac, found herself with child. The Lord told her that two nations were in her womb; two manner of people, and one people would be stronger that the other and the oldest child would serve the younger. Genesis 25:23. Soon afterward, she gave birth to twins. Esau was the first child born. The second child was Jacob.

Being the elder, Esau, by custom, was to receive the birthright, the family inheritance. The birthright, however, encompassed a very important responsibility. The eldest male was to serve as head over his brothers and exercise priestly rights on their behalf. Esau despised the responsibility of the birthright. He chose to live for instant gratification. He was reckless. Careless. Not a seeker of God's way.

As the children grew, their family became increasingly dysfunctional. Isaac and Rebekah picked favorites early in the lives of their boys. Isaac loved Esau more than Jacob. So Esau became a father pleaser. He devoted himself to the things that his father enjoyed. The outdoors. A man of the fields. Hunting dear. Eating venison. Rebekah, however, loved Jacob more than Esau. So Jacob became a mother pleaser. He liked doing the household chores with his mother. Cleaning. Cooking. Staying in the tents. As the boys grew, they became more and more distant from each other. Each had difficulty understanding the other.

Also, there was an unresolvable conflict between Isaac and Rebekah. Isaac became convinced that Esau, being the elder son, was to be given the birthright blessing as was the custom. He did not believe in the revelation that Rebekah had received from the Lord that positioned Jacob as the birthright recipient instead of Esau. Eventually, it appears that this matter became a subject that was off limits for them. They could not discuss it without becoming argumentative.

Rebekah apparently also told Jacob about the revelation she had been given from the Lord about the birthright. This caused Jacob to seek an occasion to work some kind of deal with his brother so the prophecy would come true.

One day the opportunity came for Jacob. He was sitting by some pottage that he had just prepared. Esau entered the kitchen after a long period of hunting in the field. He was faint. Weary. Exhausted. Famished. When he asked Jacob for some pottage to eat, Jacob demanded the birthright in exchange for the pottage.

Esau replied that he was about to die. At that moment the birthright seemed of little value. He took the pottage.

Jacob asked his brother to take a solemn oath concerning the deal. Esau, who despised the birthright responsibility anyway, gave Jacob an oath. Thereupon the deal was sealed. Soon Esau's belly was filled. Perhaps he thought that this deal he made with Jacob wouldn't happen anyway. That the birthright blessing would eventually be given to him anyway according to the custom. Isaac may have already told him that he would receive the birthright regardless of what Rebekah thought.

Esau's real character showed when he, in an act of self-will, married two Hittite women who were idol worshippers. His parents were both bitterly grieved by his decision.

In the course of time, Isaac became aged and blind. One day Rebekah overheard him giving instructions to Esau to hunt and prepare venison for him to eat, and afterward, he would pronounce the birthright blessing upon him. She panicked. It can't be? It mustn't be?

She had faith in the Lord's revelation to her. Jacob was to receive the birthright. But, she didn't have the faith to believe that the Lord could handle the situation. She had to help God out.

An emergency plan was hastily concocted. A plan of trickery. Deceit. Rebekah found Jacob. She quickly told him about the dilemma facing them. Then she commanded him to immediately follow her implicit directions. She told him to go to the flock of goats, choose two kids and bring them to her so she could prepare savory meat for Isaac. Jacob was then told that he would have to offer the meal to his father so he could receive the birthright blessing that Isaac was planning to give to Esau. Jacob stalled. He wondered what would happen if his father would ask to hold his hand and feel his skin. Rebekah explained that she would fasten the skins of the kids over his hands so they would feel hairy and told him to wear Esau's clothing so he would smell like Esau.

Jacob did as she requested. Isaac was suspicious of his voice, but after feeling his hairy hands and smelling the clothing that emitted the odor of the field, he became sufficiently deceived and pronounced the birthright blessing upon Jacob.

Moments after Jacob had left the presence of Isaac, Esau came with venison already prepared for his father to eat. When Isaac learned that he had been deceived, he trembled exceedingly. And Esau, tough man that he was, cried out with a bitter cry. But, the blessing had been given. It could not be retracted. Esau pleaded with his father for a blessing and wept. His father could only say that he would live by the sword and serve his brother.

Afterward, Rebekah learned that Esau intended to kill Jacob. So she told Jacob to flee to her brother's home near Haran. However, Rebekah's deceitful plan was not without severe consequence. She lost her beloved son, Jacob. She never saw him again. Twenty years passed before Jacob returned to the land of Canaan. She also lost Esau, the son whom it seems she never really had since early childhood. The pain and loneliness she felt from the absence of her boys followed her to her grave.

I can't help wondering how the events in the lives of Isaac, Rebekah and their sons would have unfolded if Rebekah's eyes had looked upward during the birthright crisis. If she had prayed, "My Lord, I know what you revealed to me regarding the birthright blessing. I'm trusting you to bring it to pass."

There is another story in the Old Testament in which God was not consulted. There was a priest of God, Abiathar, who had escaped an untimely death by the sword. He fled to David while David was still being hunted by King Saul. The story happened like this... The prophet, Gad, had warned David to flee into the land of Judah to escape the jealous wrath of King Saul. On his way, David and his company stopped at the city of Nob, the city of priests, for supplies. Ahimelech, the Priest, gave David bread and the sword of Goliath, then David fled into the forest of Hareth. Doeg, the Edomite, who was in charge over the servants of Saul, witnessed what had taken place and told King Saul what the priest had done for David. King Saul immediately pronounced a sentence of death upon Ahimelech and all of his father's house. That day, eighty-five priests were slain. Abiathar, however, a son of Ahimelech, managed to escape for his life and found David's hiding place. David consoled him saying, "Stay with me; do not fear. For he who seeks my life seeks your life, but with me you shall be safe." I Samuel 22:23.

Abiathar was used by God to direct David's decisions, thus protecting him from his enemies. He served David during his reign as King of Israel. But, alas, a time came when he acted according to his own thinking. King David was old and close to death. Adonijah, an elder half-brother of Solomon, made a move to take over his father, King David's throne. To Abiathar, Adonijah by age was favored to reign as Israel's next king, so he joined ranks with Adonijah, offered numerous sacrifices and proclaimed him king.

Nathan, the prophet of God, however, knew that Solomon was to reign upon David's throne. He informed King David of the conspiracy. Action was promptly taken to defeat Adonijah's plot and establish Solomon on the throne of his father. Abiathar, being found worthy of death, was removed from the priesthood. He spent the remainder of his life working his own fields. For many years he had carried the Ark of the Lord before King David. Then he was abruptly benched for failing to consult the mind of God. He could no longer serve as a priest of the Lord.

In 1981, after spending over eleven years working for a large electronic and electrical connector manufacturer, having responsibilities for electroplating and metal finishing, I learned that a small electroplating shop was for sale. Although I was doing well as a manager and had exposure at the corporate level, I was intrigued with the thought of going into business for myself. The shop I wanted to purchase had six employees. I saw opportunity. It was something I wanted to do. It was easy to assume that the circumstances that caused me to learn of the sale and my desire to purchase were indications of the Lord's leading. I proceeded with the purchase. Looking back on the outcome of this purchase, however, I could have saved myself a lot of grief if I had sought God's will in this matter and not proceeded with assumption.

Things went well at first. Over a period of five years, billing increased five fold. As sales increased, it became necessary to expand the operation. I purchased over four acres of ground in an industrial park and designed an electroplating facility that could accommodate an additional three fold increase in billings.

After I had committed to the project, the local sewer authority notified me that they were going to require contaminant metals discharge limits nine times lower than any of the other plating plants in the state. In an effort to comply, I purchased a top-of-the-line waste treatment system that represented the most recent technology. The waste treatment system, however, failed to consistently produce the desired results, even under the most careful conditions. The company was the state's largest cadmium electroplater, and the required discharge limit for cadmium was often exceeded. Fines were imposed at the local level. To make matters worse, negative publicity in the local papers began to take away business. Finally, the firm could no longer meet its financial obligations and I was forced to file for bankruptcy protection.

The pressures I experienced in attempting to keep the company solvent led to many additional hours at the plant. This forced me to sacrifice family time and church commitments. Obligations in serving another cause moved me toward the bench.

Our choices may lead us away from God's will to a position of uselessness. But when we again seek His direction, He leads us back to the place where we stepped from His purpose and enables us to resume climbing. The Lord guides us as we give Him full control of our circumstances and quit trying to make something happen that may not be the best for us. Knowing and following God's will for our lives is not some emotional high that comes for a moment and disappears when adversity comes. God's plan for us becomes significant when we decide to follow His leading. Then, as a caring Shepherd, He guides us through the progression of our circumstances, prompting us by His Spirit to make decisions concerning personal choices, education and ministry that moves us from the bench and propels us to new heights.

We need to learn to rely on the Shepherd of our souls:

> To show us who we are,
> To show us our calling,
> To lead us into the will of God, and
> To assure us that in His name we have been given all power and authority.

Jesus was sent by God into this world for a divine purpose. He did not take it upon himself to come into the world. He was appointed and commissioned by God. Jesus came to earth knowing His calling. He has gone before us. He knows the way. Indeed, He is the way.

We do well to consult our Heavenly Father earnestly in regard to every decision we face. To presume that we know what is best is to invite a position on the bench.

*IF A PERSON REALLY
LOVES ME,
HE WILL KEEP MY WORD
AND OBEY MY TEACHING;
AND MY FATHER
WILL LOVE HIM,
AND WE WILL COME AND
MAKE OUR HOME WITH HIM.
JOHN 14:23, TAB.*

Frank H Leaman

Disobeying God's Directives

Many times, we, as the children of God, become benched for disobeying the directives of God. His desires for us do not please us. We insist on choosing our own way of living and serving Him or we choose to not serve Him at all. At times, following our own way blinds us to the truth that our work for God is actually bringing dishonor to Him, hindering His work more than helping it and damaging our relationship with God.

Disobeying God's directives is an act of sin. Refusal to trust God and follow His leading is a signal of rebellion and pride. The sin we pursue blocks the presence and power of God in our lives and leaves us exposed to the forces of evil. It can create massive havoc and rob us of lasting joy and peace. It places a wedge between us and our Creator and blocks the fellowship God desires to have with us. Often we don't regard sin as much of an issue; but it is, and its ultimate sting is eternal death and separation from God. A high price to pay for momentary satisfaction and fleeting pleasure.

All sin originates in the mind as temptation. The temptation does not become sin unless we yield to it. The temptation awaits our moment of decision. Saying *no* to sin keeps us in God's presence and within His protection. Saying *yes* causes us to become unfaithful in our devotion to God. Committing sin puts us under the mastership of Satan, whose primary goal is to bench believers and make their walk with God ineffective and even impossible.

Our disobedience toward God can grow through the process of convincing ourselves that God wants us to move in a direction that we feel we would really like to take. Sometimes we want something so badly and pray so fervently that we don't realize the power our own will is exerting in a matter that greatly concerns us. Eventually, we can be misled to believe that what we want, God wants too.

Self-will plagued the first child to be born on earth, and at times has been a trademark of us all. Cain was instructed by his parents concerning the method of sacrifice to God for atonement and forgiveness of sins. For our cleansing, the law of God is unchanging. His word instructs us that shed blood makes atonement for the soul and without the shedding of blood there is no remission of sins. Yet Cain, a proficient gardener who took great pride in the results of his cunning and toil, chose to offer vegetables tilled by his hands to God upon altars of fire rather than animal sacrifices as God had prescribed. Genesis 4:3. As a sign of God's rejection to Cain, the smoke from his vegetable sacrifices flowed downward along the ground rather than ascending toward the heavens.

Unwilling to settle his problem of self-will with God, Cain stubbornly insisted on having his own way. Soon, self-will festered and grew into deep jealousy and hatred toward his brother. At a moment of opportunity, Cain slew his brother Abel, whose animal sacrifices had been accepted by God, and buried his body beneath the field.

But the Lord called to Cain from the heavens concerning his evil act. Cain was benched in an act of judgment. The earth became cursed for him and no longer produced a full yield for him. His fate was that of a fugitive and a vagabond. He was driven from his home.

A prophet in Old Testament times also disobeyed the directions God had given him. Jonah 1:3. Jonah was instructed to go to Nineveh and warn the inhabitants of that great trade city that their evil would soon result in calamity and destruction unless they repented. Jonah made a determined decision to act contrary to God's command. The people of Ninevah were his enemies. He fled in the opposite direction, and boarded a ship headed to Tarshish. Soon he found himself benched. A violent storm threatened to destroy the ship. By Jonah's own request, in a noble effort to save the crew and passengers from sinking into the raging sea, he instructed the sailors to cast him overboard.

God prepared a great fish to provide a temporary home for Jonah. While Jonah didn't consider this an act of God's mercy at first, it did provide him time to sort out his thoughts and come to a position of repentance. Then, and only then, did he again become an instrument that God could use to fulfill His purpose.

After three days in the belly of the fish, Jonah was vomited onto the shore. He washed himself and headed for Nineveh in haste. He was recharged, filled with power from God and committed to fulfill the mission to which he had been assigned.

Our Heavenly Father cannot overlook our willful disobedience to His directives. To do so would be totally against His character and nature. In acts of love too deep for us to fathom, He operates consistently with His justice and mercy in discipline to bring us to repentance and usefulness. We respond to His grace.

> Our pain becomes gain.
> Our confusion becomes focused conviction.
> Our unproductiveness becomes renewed dedication to our
> Master's work.

How beautifully and carefully God deals with us! How much He wins our hearts!

Sometimes our disobedience to God is a gradual process that overtakes us subtly rather than in a decisive act. The failures of one generation can lead to the fall of the next generation. Joshua, Moses' successor as leader of the children of Israel, and the people he led, failed in the mission the Lord had given them in two critical ways.

God had commanded the Israelites to drive out the idolatrous inhabitants in the land of Canaan so that their evil would not lead Israel into sin. But, God's people became weary with this pursuit. The tribes of Israel chose to settle down on their territorial claims. They permitted some of the heathen to live among them. The Israelites chose to profit from the remaining inhabitants by taxing them. Later, this profiteering became their curse. The children of Israel intermarried with the Canaanites, the Jebusites, the Asherites and the Amorites and followed after their gods.

Secondly, they failed to diligently instruct their young in the ways of God. When Joshua and the elders who served with him died, knowledge of the great acts that Jehovah had wrought for His people began to die also. The next generation didn't know the Lord and the works that He had done for Israel. The failures of one generation caused the deprivation, suffering and benching of the next generation. How tragic!

The book of Judges records the disunion that plagued God's people. The key verse in Judges, "Every man did that which was right in his own eyes," shows the Israelites' condition and gives the reason for their perpetual failures. During a period of three hundred five years, the Lord raised up judges to deliver Israel from misery and oppression. Cycles of cursing and blessing coinciding with their sin and repentance were repeated seven times. On the bench, then off the bench. One generation blessed and the next one cursed and impoverished. What a lesson for us today! We, to a great degree, hold in our hands the fate of our children and our children's children. We need to be sincere and faithful in teaching them about God.

Disobedience is a matter of choice. When we fail to walk in obedience to God's word, it is not because we do not have power over sin, nor because we do not have control over our actions. This is why we disobey:

> We yield to our own will.
> We willfully reject God's word.
> We willfully oppose God and His authority over us.

The alternative is to choose to obey. In making that choice, we are promised that sin will lose its power over us. We will enjoy victory and experience God's blessings. We will become free to yield ourselves to God, using our resources and gifts to walk in His light and see His glory.

This is the spiritual territory that God has planned for us:

> Living in a cycle of victory with the power of God flowing through us.
> Pressing on to perfection.
> Growing into the full stature of Jesus Christ.

Jesus walked the way of obedience before us. He steadfastly and determinedly set His face to go to Jerusalem, knowing that He would be crucified. In the garden of Gethsemane, He relinquished His desire to escape, becoming the world's sin bearer to do His Father's will. In the cold darkness of that garden, we can hear Jesus pleading with His Father, "Please provide some other way. I don't know how I can go through with your plan for me."

But His Father's answer assured Him that He alone was the perfect one without blemish. The only acceptable sacrifice to atone for the sins of mankind and establish their redemption.

"Father," Jesus cried, "My flesh is so weak. The pain and suffering will be so intense. And the weight of all of the world's sins will be so much more unbearable." Drops of sweat mixed with blood. An agony not known to mortal men.

His Father suffered anguish too. From His throne room in Heaven, when the world's sins were transferred upon His beloved Son, He turned His back, unable to watch Jesus sacrificed and dying. He would hear His Son's heart rending cry, "My God, why have you forsaken me?" Matthew 27:46. He felt the pain as Jesus did.

In the consumption of the struggle, Jesus gave Heaven the answer that became His sacrificial death and our triumph, "Not my will, but thine be done."

Jesus yielded to the cruel whims of the mocking soldiers as they tore at His beard, beat him, spat upon Him, and pressed a crown of thorns into His head. He suffered the nails that were driven through His hands and feet and the hours of agony hanging on a suspended cross while His life's blood drained from Him and His bones loosened from their joints. But more than all of this. Yes, much more. The moment in time came when the sins of all mankind were cast upon Him. Our sin bearer. That's how we know Him. The Lamb of God. Our Savior. Our Redeemer. The Father who would become our Father, turned away and wept, then wiped His tears, sighed, and finally smiled. He could see the day when Heaven's Courts would ring with the singing of the justified. The glorified. Persons once mortal who accepted His gift and had their sins cleansed by the precious blood of His Beloved Son.

Jesus learned obedience. Through His obedience He was perfected. He became the author of eternal salvation for us. The road of obedience Jesus walked was a daily experience with God.

> Fasting and praying to know His Father's will.
> A burning desire to do God's will regardless of the cost.
> An awesome respect for His Father.
> A fervent love for mankind.

In order for us to follow Jesus, we need to walk on the road of obedience to the Father's will, having hearing ears to hear His voice and a wholesome fear of the Righteous and Holy God we serve.

In the model prayer, Jesus said we are to pray to our Father, "Thy will be done on earth as it is in heaven."

This petition implies that we recognize that God's will is supreme and we desire to have His will done. It implies a delight in having the will of God done by all His creatures. In his book *Prevailing Prayer,*

Charles G. Finney wrote, "The honest-hearted suppliant is as willing that God's will should be done as the saints in heaven are. His heart will acquiesce both in the things required and in the manner in which God requires them."

Praying this prayer sincerely means that we are desirous of doing the will of God. It also implies a willingness that God should use His own discretion in the affairs of the universe. In this world as well as in heaven.

Finney described the state of feeling that the heavenly creatures have toward God. "There, all created beings exercise the most perfect submission and confidence in God. They all allow Him to carry out His own plans, framed in wisdom and love, and they even rejoice with exceeding joy that He does. It is their highest blessing."

So our highest blessing becomes a conformity of life to God's will and purpose. We each pray with all earnestness, "Thy will be done in and through my life. In me."

As we struggle together in our humanness, nothing is more pathetic then the failure to recover from a fall when a way is available for recovery. But mankind is so vulnerable to deciding "I will" and "I will not," that sometimes there is failure to recognize that either of these choices can lead to a terrible fall.

We are told in the scriptures that Lucifer, the son of the morning, whose abode was among the angels of heaven, made an "I will" decision to follow his own ulterior motives instead of the will of God. He actually attempted a rebellion against God in heaven and was cast out.

We are also told of an incident that occurred during the time that the Israelites wandered in the wilderness when some of the people made an "I will not" decision. Numbers 21. God sent poisonous snakes among them because of their bitter complaining about the tasteless monotony of the meal of manna God provided for them to eat each day. They didn't realize that the manna miraculously contained all the salt, vitamins and minerals their bodies needed for their sustenance in the desert. As the bitten began to die, a cry of repentance arose. God instructed Moses to place a serpent of brass on a pole in the middle of the assembly. The serpent was erected. Dispatchers were hastily sent in every direction to tell the dying to look at the brass serpent and they would be healed. Many looked and were healed instantly. But others in bitterness and hatred put their faces to the ground and said, "I will not look." Unlike their fellows who believed and beheld salvation, they perished and their bodies were buried in the sand.

Later in Israel's history, when Saul was chosen to be the first King of Israel, the Bible says that he was "a choice young man and there was not among the children of Israel a goodlier person than he; and from his shoulders and upward he was taller than any of the people." I Samuel 9:2.

Early in his reign as King, Saul demonstrated qualities of humility, a willingness to withstand mistreatment and a spirit that did not seek revenge. When he heard that the Ammonites were coming to war against him, the Spirit of the Lord came upon him and he took a yoke of oxen and cut them in pieces. Then he sent the pieces throughout Israel with the message, "Whoever does not come out after Saul and after Samuel, so shall it be done to his oxen." I Samuel 11:7.

The people responded in fear with one consent. Three hundred thirty thousand came. They went against the Ammonites and fought them until no two of them remained together.

But two years later, another enemy came. The Philistines gathered against Israel with thirty thousand chariots and a multitude of soldiers. Some of the Israelites fled over the Jordan River. Others hid in caves, pits and thickets, trembling for their lives. I Samuel 13:6.

King Saul received a message from God that he should wait seven days for the Prophet Samuel to come and offer sacrifices. On the seventh day, Samuel still had not appeared and Saul's impatience under the threatening circumstances took over. Saul offered the burnt offering himself. As soon as he finished this act, Samuel arrived at the altar. He rebuked Saul for foolishly failing to keep the commandment of the Lord. Samuel told Saul that very day that the Lord would look for another to reign in his stead because of his disobedience. But God remained faithful to his people Israel and wrought a marvelous victory for them. He sent a severe earthquake that confused and terrified the enemy until they slew each other in their desperation to flee.

Soon the word of the Lord came to Samuel saying, "Saul has turned back from following me and has not performed my commandments." I Samuel 15:11. Samuel eventually had to tell Saul,

"The Lord has rent the kingdom from you and has given it to a neighbor who is better than you."

Then the Philistines came against Israel again. Saul sought out a woman who was a fortune teller to ask what he should do. He was told that the Philistines would win the battle. As the armies were fighting, King Saul was struck with an arrow. He realized that he was going to die. Not wanting to die at the hands of the enemy, he fell upon his sword.

Saul's fall from the bench didn't occur as the sword cut through his body. He fell from the bench when the Spirit of the Lord departed from him. We are warned in God's word that "God's Spirit will not always strive with man." Genesis 6:3.

There can come a time in our retreat from the playing field when we lose all desire to play the game by God's directives and we deliberately disown Him. In doing so, we become the possession of another master. The Apostle Peter described this master as our enemy, a roaring lion seeking to devour. A lion roars when its paws are resting on its prey. King Saul ended up under the lion's paws. He paid the extreme price for disobedience. The truth of the matter is, his life didn't have to end this way. The good news of the Gospel is that God's grace is always available to us, even during our worst times. All that is required for God's presence to flood our lives anew is our willingness to forsake our sin and accept His cleansing and forgiveness.

THE SPIRIT OF THE LORD
IS UPON ME,
BECAUSE HE HAS
ANOINTED ME
TO PREACH THE GOSPEL
TO THE POOR;
HE HAS SENT ME TO HEAL
THE BROKENHEARTED —-
TO SET AT LIBERTY
THOSE WHO ARE OPPRESSED.
LUKE 4:18.

Hurt

We all have our times of trouble. In fact, trouble seems to be experienced by every living thing.

Chippy was a parakeet that suffered from an accident that was not his fault. His trouble was the direct result of his owner who forgot to close his cage door, then later decided to clean the drapes with a vacuum cleaner. In the process of running the brush attachment across the top of one of the drapes, Chippy's owner was horrified to see Chippy sucked into the attachment. A quick look at the attachment confirmed the worst. Chippy had been sucked down the hose. His owner frantically opened the vacuum cleaner and tore open the dirt collection bag. In a moment, Chippy was found with dust and dirt all over him. He looked a mess! His owner promptly ran to the kitchen sink and doused him with cold water to wash the dirt away. Chippy's little body began to shiver, so his owner ran to the bathroom, grabbed a hair dryer and dried him as quickly as she could. Then Chippy was properly secured in his cage. He was so stunned and disturbed by the ordeal that for three days he just sat and stared and wouldn't sing. He had lost his song.

There are times in life's experiences when tragedy strikes with sudden cruelty. Like an avalanche, it can sweep away a lover, a parent, a child or a cherished friend. Accidents can maim and cripple us. Disease can pull us tenaciously toward the brink of death. We become paralyzed by hurt. Haunted by darkness of night that refuses to break into day. Broken. Suffering. Sometimes fearful. Sometimes angry. Longing for answers to our questions. Trauma moves deeply within our souls and takes a bitter toll.

These times of trouble are often unexpected and undeserved. The pain of trouble, the fear and the agony of not knowing why can force us into isolation and aloneness. In the midst of trouble, we can either groan for a glimpse of God's face or we can complain in bitterness and blame God for our plight. If we in such times fail to let go of the pain and hurt, bitterness will overcome us and drive us into depression and despair. Our entire lives can be distorted by holding onto pain. We conclude that others don't want to see our crying eyes or listen to our questions or sympathize with us.

137

But when we hurt the worst, we need the body of Christ the most. We need to remember that we have a God who cares about us and understands how we feel, a God who loves us with an infinite love and who grieves with us, a God who has promised never to forsake us, and a God that provides us with His comfort and peace. He is the answer to our aloneness. Yielding to His enablement lifts us from our deserts and valleys to the mountain tops. There are those among us who would readily testify that their marks of tragedy, their losses and their crosses have enabled them to serve God more effectively than would have been possible otherwise. This often proves true for God's children who have been hurt the most and who ultimately become the most loving and caring.

Henry Bosch, in his book *Rainbows for God's Children in the Storm,* reminds us, "Christians often learn more in times of darkness and trial than in the pleasant sunlight of prosperity. God may be shrouded in a thick, impenetrable cloud when He has something very important to teach us. Yet we will not enjoy the treasures of His grace until we master the lessons He brings us in those gloomy days of distress. Even when we feel forsaken, God is near. We ought to approach our difficulties without flinching. Beyond the blackness of our most severe trial, God's special blessing awaits us."

Also Bosch wrote some thoughts that Pastor Troy Corzine observed, "The crushed rose gives off the sweetest fragrance, and the pains of childbirth are compensated by the joys of motherhood. A grain of sand makes a wound in the body of an oyster, and yet from that irritation a lovely pearl is formed. Indeed, many of the beauties of Heaven will be fashioned from the bruises of earth!"

I like the words J.B. Phillips used when he paraphrased the second verse in James, chapter two - "When all kinds of trials and failures crowd into your lives, my brothers, don't resent them as intruders, but welcome them as friends. Realize that they come to test your faith and produce in you the quality of endurance."

Another kind of hurt we sometimes experience results from mistreatment inflicted by selfish and mean-spirited people. We feel the instant pain of heartache and disappointment deep within. Someone is rewarded a promotion that we are more deserving of because another was willing to compromise a moral standard. A spouse is dealt the cutting knife of betrayal. An innocent person's life becomes upset by an act of prejudice. And who has not felt the sting of being unjustly ridiculed, slandered or falsely accused? Such incidences springing so suddenly into our lives ravish our physical, emotional and spiritual fortitude. The damage is real and it sends us reeling.

Once dealt the blow, we drop what we were doing and stagger toward the bench. The reaction is similar to receiving a punch to the stomach and having the wind knocked out of us. Feelings mushroom within and strive to overtake us. Embarrassment, humiliation, abandonment, rejection, fear and even anger. Recovery might come soon, or it may never come. The choice is ours.

Prolonged emotional and spiritual damage doesn't result from the hurt itself. Lasting harm can only come to us if we allow the hurt to breed within us an unforgiving spirit and hatred toward the offender. If the hurt we feel gives way to bitterness and a desire to get even, we will eventually put ourselves into a bed of suffering. Our ability to give and receive love will wane.

When suffering hurt that others have inflicted upon us, we really only have two options: to forgive the offender or to not forgive. Complete forgiveness is the only cure for a hurting heart. The power of forgiveness thrusts us forward and upward in spirit and enables us to function as before. Although harboring a feeling of revenge is a choice more easily made, it is also the choice that chains us to the bench.

Philemon was converted to Christianity by the Apostle Paul. He lived in Colosse, a small city in Asia Minor that at that time was part of the Roman Empire. One day, to his dismay, he learned that a slave of his, Onesimus, had stolen some of his goods and had fled the city. Onesimus, if caught, by Roman Law would have been under a penalty of death. But he fled to Rome and Philemon didn't know where he had gone.

We can readily imagine the frustration and disappointment Philemon felt. There is nothing to suggest that he was a harsh master. Rather, Paul wrote in a very complimentary manner that he had heard of Philemon's love toward the Lord and his fellowmen. Philemon had been gracious and fair. He certainly didn't deserve the treatment he was dealt by Onesimus.

In Rome, Onesimus, who was unemployed and without family, was befriended by the Christians. Eventually, he was introduced to Paul who was in prison. Under Paul's ministry, Onesimus became converted. Paul took time to instruct Onesimus in the Gospel. But a time came when Paul asked Onesimus to return to Philemon. He slipped a brief letter into his hands and told him to deliver it to Philemon. In the letter, Paul instructed Philemon to do more than accept Onesimus as a servant. Paul asked him to consider Onesimus as a brother beloved and in the Lord.

Paul ended this letter with the words, "The grace of our Lord Jesus Christ be with your spirit." I like that. Forgiveness is conceived deep within our spirit. And forgiveness that embraces acceptance is born from a spirit that has been bathed in the grace of God.

Children are very vulnerable to being hurt. Often the rules of the adult world are harshly applied to them without the expression of love and caring. Particularly when a child is unable to understand a decision or an action that has impacted him, a genuine spirit of concern for his well-being is essential.

I remember one time when I became very hurt emotionally as a child. Part way through third grade, I was transferred to a new school. I felt lost. Everyone else was familiar with the scheduled activities and knew where things were, but I was not. Although the new school was closer to my home, I had to spend forty-five minutes on the bus, then walk a half mile on a farmer's lane and cross a cow pasture to get home. After riding the bus for several days, I decided to walk home. It was a rather cold October day. I buried my hands deep within my coat pockets and began walking on the sidewalk. Before I had left the school grounds, I was suddenly tackled from behind by another boy who had become somewhat bored with the lack of activity in a football game. I went down so quickly I was unable to get my hands out of my pockets. My face hit the curb. I saw a spark jump as two of my upper front teeth broke in half.

The next day, according to my parent's instructions, I reported the incident to my teacher and asked if the school would pay to have my teeth repaired. She sent me to the principal's office. This was my first encounter with the principal. Intimidated by her harsh retort, "What do <u>you</u> want?", I mustered all the courage I could and told her my problem and the need for money to get my teeth fixed. In response, she abruptly rose from her chair and yelled, "You dumb stupid child. You were supposed to ride the bus home. If I ever catch you walking home again, I'll lay a board to your behind. This school can't pay you for anything. Now get out of my office. Go back to your classroom."

I wasn't used to being treated so disrespectfully. My parents disciplined me firmly, but with love. Her unjust cruelty toward me raised both terror and hatred. I was frightened to walk in the halls. The bitterness I felt inhibited my concentration in the classroom.

Then I remembered a Sunday School lesson about forgiveness that brought relief to my young heart. Seventy times seven. I didn't know how big that number was, but I knew it was big. Yes. If that is what Jesus wanted me to do, I would do it. I prayed about it. Forgiveness happened. I never spoke to the principal again, but when I saw her, my little mind would say, "I forgave you."

God is with us in our hurts. We only need to recognize Him. When we get hurt, He is already aware of it. And He meets us in proportion to our needs. Our darkness is dispelled with His glorious presence. He is the healer of the broken hearted. The Psalmist declared, "The Lord is near to those who have a broken heart." Psalm 34:18. What consolation to realize that we are not alone! Even in our pain and loneliness, we can feel the touch of God. We can grow in our relationship with Him. We are not forsaken.

The key to bearing our sufferings and hurt is couched in recognizing the greatness and the sovereignty of our God. Feeling His presence. Being encompassed with His love. Believing that He is our El-Shaddai, our All Sufficient One. Not seeking what God can do for us, but what He can to through us. The joy that comes in the morning is in the bearing of fruit that adversity has no power to destroy.

In our worst experiences, God in His mercy reaches from His throne room desiring to lift our heads. He wants us to know that He is sovereign. That we will never completely understand the reasons for our hurt until we stroll with Him in glory. He wants us to know that He is still our hope, our provider, our shield, our strong tower. That He knows our pain and that He hurts with us. That His supply of love and grace is inexhaustible. That His storehouse of provision is always full. That our mornings will always come. As God's children, we will have our day of resurrection! And no trouble on earth can prevent that!

The Apostle Paul stressed the great comfort we have in knowing our Heavenly Father this way.

"Blessed be God … the God of all comfort, who comforts us in all our affliction, so that we may be able to comfort

141

those who are in any affliction, with the comfort with which we ourselves are comforted by God." II Corinthians 1:3,4.

Sufficient comfort for any trouble. A healer of broken hearts. That's the kind of God we have. Why, then, should we allow our hurts to bench us and keep us from serving Him?

*FOR IF YOU FORGIVE MEN
THEIR TRESPASSES,
YOUR HEAVENLY FATHER
WILL ALSO FORGIVE YOU:
BUT IF YOU FORGIVE NOT
MEN THEIR TRESPASSES,
NEITHER WILL YOUR FATHER
FORGIVE YOUR TRESPASSES.
MATTHEW 6:14, 15.*

Failure to Forgive

An unforgiving and bitter spirit can easily be hidden deep within us away from the observation of others. It can slowly fester and grow. It can even lie in a dormant state for many years, but if not reconciled, sometime when there is occasion, it will strike in swiftness and inject deadly poison into its prey. Our feelings of unforgiveness can be directed against our God as well as others. While others may be hurt in the strike, we do untold damage to ourselves as well. By reliving the hurt for weeks, months, even years afterward, disharmony and bitterness smother us like a heavy blanket and our souls dry up.

To paraphrase a statement written by Ann Landers, "Unforgiveness hurts those in which it is stored more than it hurts those on whom it is poured."

We deal best with destructive thoughts and feelings that are unforgiving by learning to forgive the offender and perhaps even learning to forgive ourselves. There is tremendous resource to forgive an offender when we ponder how much forgiveness our God has extended to us. Remaining unwilling or unable to forgive invites disaster.

Our self image becomes blurred when we don't forgive others and don't feel forgiven ourselves. Feelings of guilt, shame and worthlessness can drive a wedge between us and other people and can even separate us from God. Our own health and well-being can suffer considerable damage from the bitterness that results by harboring an unforgiving spirit. No one, ourselves included, can do anything that is too awful to be forgiven.

Ahithophel was King David's counselor. II Samuel 15. The Scriptures tell us that his counsel was so perfect it was as though he inquired at the very oracles of God. However, he was also the grandfather of Bathsheba, the woman with whom King David committed adultery and whose husband King David had ordered to be slain. For many years, Ahithophel secretly harbored an unforgiving spirit against his king. Finally, during the fortieth year of David's reign, an opportunity arose for Ahithophel to get even with David.

Unknown to David, Absalom, his oldest son, began a conspiracy to overthrow his throne. He sent spies throughout all the land to sound trumpets to proclaim him king. Ahithophel joined ranks with

145

Absalom. Upon hearing of the conspiracy, King David fled in haste from his palace. Many of the people supported Absalom.

In the pain, horror and blackness of this calamity, David realized that a son he loved had rebelled against him and wanted him killed to take over his throne. Sought for death, David turned to his God. His rock of salvation. His fortress. His deliverer. His only hope. Samuel, the prophet, vividly described David's pleas to God.

> "And David went up by the ascent of mount olivet, and wept as he went up, and had his head covered, and he went barefoot: and all the people that were with him covered every man his head, and they went up, weeping as they went up. And one told David, saying, Ahithophel is among the conspirators with Absalom. And David said, O Lord, I pray thee, turn the counsel of Ahithophel into foolishness."

The knowledge of Ahithophel's betrayal immediately invoked David to pray to God. In the midst of his tragedy, David realized that Ahithophel would counsel his own son, Absalom, to have him slain.

The answer to David's prayer came swiftly. When David reached the top of the mount, Hushai, a young man who also had been a counselor in David's court, came to meet him, greatly distressed. David asked him to return to the city of Jerusalem and align himself with Absalom so the Lord could use him to defeat the counsel of Ahithophel.

David's cry of fear and hurt is uttered in Psalm 55.

> "Give ear to my prayer, O God; and do not hide yourself from my supplication. Attend to me, and hear me: I am restless in my complaint, and moan noisily, because of the voice of the enemy, because of the oppression of the wicked: for they bring down trouble upon me, and in wrath they hate me. My heart is severely pained within me, and the terrors of death have fallen upon me. Fearfulness and trembling have come upon me, and horror has overwhelmed me. For it is not an enemy who reproaches me; But it was you, a man my equal, my guide, and my acquaintance. We took sweet counsel together, and walked to the house of God in the throng."

What searing hurt it is to be betrayed by a trusted friend! Especially one that you enjoyed sweet fellowship with and worshipped with. But David took his pain and his hurt and his fear to the Lord and trusted his keeping to the Rock of his Salvation.

When Absalom entered the palace in Jerusalem, Ahithophel was asked to give counsel. The depth of his unforgiveness toward David for defiling his granddaughter years before sprung to light in evil counsel. He instructed Absalom to seal his position before the people by spreading a tent on the palace roof in the sight of all Israel and go into the tent with David's concubines. The very sin he hated David for, he advised another to commit in a ten fold way. Absalom readily accepted his counsel and the wickedness was committed.

Then Ahithophel requested that Absalom give him twelve thousand men to pursue David that night. He said, "I will come upon him while he is weary and weak handed and the people with him will flee and I will smite the king only." II Samuel 17:2. So great was his hatred. Within him it had seethed and grown year after year until it could no longer be contained.

Absalom, however, also sought additional counsel from Hushai. Hushai counseled that all Israel be gathered together in battle and advised that Absalom should lead them in person to find and slay David. Absalom chose the counsel of Hushai. That choice gave David an opportunity to build a defense and prepare for battle. Ahithophel, wise as he was, knew that giving David time was a certain mistake. He knew that David would victoriously return to the throne. He would not be able to face David. He went to his home and hung himself. It was an act of permanent benching. From an unforgiving heart, he had thrown a dagger that circled like a boomerang and pierced his own soul.

A pastor once told me of an incident he experienced where a non-forgiving spirit resulted in broken fellowship. His wife had become a close friend with a lady whom she had led to the Lord. They shared many hours in prayer together through the years. But a time came when her friend became very cold and unresponsive toward her. Even deliberately so. Every approach was quickly brushed away. The rejection hurt. The minister's wife could not learn from her friend what had happened to cause the break in fellowship. The pastor and his wife kept praying that fellowship would be restored.

But the coldness continued. Finally, the friend experienced a nervous breakdown. The pastor was called a number of times by the family to pray for her. After months of suffering painful depression, the woman confessed to the pastor the deep feelings of anger and resentment she was holding against him.

Several years earlier, the pastor, knowing the financial burden that was upon this woman who was raising her family without a husband, had offered to pay her winter's coal bill to lighten her load. He ordered the coal, paid the bill, and the coal was delivered to her basement.

The pastor, however, was not aware that a bill for coal used during the previous winter had not been paid. The family began to secretly accuse the pastor of lying because he had failed to pay the outstanding coal bill. A misunderstanding had occurred. Resentment grew. Fellowship was broken. Finally, feelings intensified and caused incredible depression.

Upon the woman's confession, the misunderstanding was clarified. The healing balm of forgiveness flowed freely. In a matter of minutes she was released from her prison of anger and depression. She traded the bench for fellowship and new found joy.

We must forgive all who wrong us, and forgive them from the heart. God requires us to love our enemies as strongly as we love our friends. To forgive others to the extent that we desire to be forgiven. To have a state of mind that is genuinely forgiving toward all who may have wronged us.

True forgiving is not forgetting. We cannot erase our memory banks. Lewis B. Smedes wrote in his book, *Forgive and Forget: Healing the Hurts We Don't Deserve*, "The really important thing is that we have the power to forgive what we still do remember. And we can be healed of the pain it has left behind."

Lewis Smedes mentioned four stages that we travel through to achieve the climax of reconciliation.

> "The first stage is hurt: when somebody causes us pain so deep and unfair that we cannot forgive it, we are pushed into the first stage of the crisis of forgiving. Forgiving is love's remedy to be used when we are hurtfully wronged by a person we trusted to treat us right.

The second stage is hate: we cannot shake the memory of how much we were hurt and we want those who hurt us to suffer as we are suffering. Hate, admitted and felt, compels us to make a decision about the healing miracle of forgiving. When we deny our hate we detour around the crisis of forgiveness.

The third stage is healing: we are given the "magic eyes" to see the person who hurt us in a new light. Our memory is healed. We turn back the flow of pain and are free again. True forgivers do not pretend they don't suffer. They do not pretend the wrong does not matter much. Magic eyes are open eyes. We know that forgiveness has begun when we recall those who hurt us and feel the power to wish them well.

The fourth stage is the coming together. We invite the person who hurt us back into our lives. If he or she comes honestly, love can move toward a new and healed relationship. The fourth stage depends on the person we forgive as much as it depends on us. Sometimes the person forgiven doesn't come back and we must heal alone."

It is critical that we, as the children of God, live free from a spirit of unforgiveness. In the model prayer of Jesus, He told His followers that they should pray for God to forgive them as they forgive others. Mark 11:25, 26. An unforgiving spirit blocks our prayers and makes our service to God ineffective.

Forgiving is an unending process. "Seventy times seven," Jesus said. Matthew 18:22. He even commanded us to forgive our enemies and persecutors. Matthew 5:44.

Why? Because there is a healing balm in forgiveness. It prepares the way for wholeness. For right relationships, for fellowship with our God and each other. It is the only way to effectively play in the game.

Frank H Leaman

HE WHO IS GREEDY FOR GAIN TROUBLES HIS OWN HOUSE. PROVERBS 15:27.

Frank H Leaman

Greed

Greed begins in us quite innocently. Just a thought. A desire for something.

> Recognition.
> Popularity.
> Power.
> A better job.
> Wealth.

And the reasons for our desires are easily justified. In fact, quite proper.

> We would be asked to sing the National Anthem at the football game.
> We would be picked to serve on the Student Council.
> We would be able to put the neighborhood bully in his place.
> We would be able to give more money to the church.

Just dreams. Good ones. Not bad ones. Goals all of us should set for ourselves. Perhaps.

But when does an innocent dream for something begin to change into greed for something? When we begin to believe that we must make our dream become a reality. When we convince ourselves that we must have it. By our very nature, a desire can easily become our master. Our time, energy, resources and even our morality and convictions can be subtly torn from the things in life that really count and be sacrificed upon the altar of greed often without our even realizing what is happening. And when the dream is finally achieved, we are still left feeling unfulfilled. The late John Paul Getty, recognized as one of the world's richest men, was once asked, "How much does it take for a man to be satisfied?"

He replied, "Just a little bit more." Such is our dilemma. Our dreams are illusive. The fulfillment of our dreams often leaves us feeling unfulfilled.

In offering some sound advice, Jesus admonished His followers to seek the Kingdom of God and His righteousness first, and the other

153

necessities of life like things to eat, drink and wear would be added to them. Matthew 6:25-34. Jesus did not condone self-serving attitudes. Greatness in God's kingdom is a matter of generosity and submitting to God's way of doing things. This is the action that brings eternal reward. The primary goal of God's children should not be to live excessively. Instead, our focus should be on living lives as ministers of the Gospel in the world, serving one another.

A number of years ago, I taught a Bible study class at a low security satellite camp for persons who committed minor offenses. One of the Christian brothers who faithfully attended, was a man I called Big John because he was massive in size compared to myself. He always flashed a wide grin and had the joy of the Lord in his heart.

One day I asked him if he had been a Christian prior to his sentence. He replied that he had been, but not a good one. He told me he had stopped following the leading of the Lord in his life.

As a result, he eventually found himself deeply entangled in a life of debauchery and sin. I asked him what he felt was the primary cause for his fall. He looked at me intently, then replied, "Greed."

John had gradually built several successful businesses in his area. Scrap metal. Dump trucks. Fire extinguisher sales and maintenance. In time his love for God became sacrificed for greed, for wealth and pleasure, nightclubs and women.

As part of this exchange, an opportunity came along for him to contract and arrange big name entertainment events in prominent cities. On a typical weekend, he could clear as much as ten thousand dollars. He began living high and dangerously.

Then John made the mistake of loaning an employee a sizeable sum of money that the employee needed to use to cover a drug deal. Authorities, suspicious of drug trafficking, had bugged John's office. Although John had never taken or sold drugs personally, he became implicated in criminal activity and was sentenced to serve time.

But John had a vibrant testimony. He explained that although he suffered much financial loss, he was grateful that he had been sentenced. During his confinement, he rededicated his life to the Lord and began to take Bible correspondence courses. He showed me nine certificates he had received for courses already completed. Then he told me in sincerity, "I know if the Lord hadn't stopped me in my pursuit of evil, I would have AIDS by now. I have much to thank God for."

At the close of Israel's wanderings in the wilderness, Moses sent messengers to Sihon, King of the Amorites, requesting permission to pass through his country on the King's Highway so the Israelites could enter the land of Canaan. Numbers 21. A promise was given that they would remain on the highway, and would not turn into the fields and vineyards. In swift response, King Sihon gathered his army together and charged into the wilderness to crush the Israelites. In the battle that ensued, King Sihon's army was defeated. So Israel took possession of the land of the Amorites.

In the neighboring country, Balak, King of the Moabites, became terrified. He thought the Israelites would invade his country next. So he sought out a prophet of God with the intention of hiring him to place a curse on the people of Israel. He sent a delegation laden with gifts to the house of Balaam. When they found Balaam, they told him how King Balak wanted him to curse the Israelites.

But the Lord met with Balaam in Israel's defense. Balaam was instructed not to go with the King's ambassadors and not to curse the Israelites. He recognized God's voice and he honored God's authority. He informed the delegation, "Return to your land. The Lord has refused me to leave with you." Numbers 22:13. The delegation left without him, taking the presents with them, but all Balaam's vision could focus on was the missed opportunity.

When King Balak was told of Balaam's refusal, he upped the ante. He dispatched his princes again with more gifts! Greed began to possess Balaam. He desired the fortune and honor of King Balak more than he desired to follow the will of God. So he saddled his donkey.

On the way, Balaam's donkey balked and pressed his leg against a wall of rock. Balaam beat the donkey. The donkey spoke like a human and asked, "Why are you beating me?". Balaam's eyes were finally opened. He saw what had frightened his donkey. An angel of the Lord was standing before him with a drawn sword. The angel told Balaam, "If your donkey had not stopped, you surely would have been slain." The angel gave him permission to continue his journey, but warned him to only speak the words that God would give him to speak.

So Balaam had his meeting with King Balak. Together they made plans to ascend into the mountains, build altars and offer sacrifices of bullocks and rams, then curse the children of Israel. But each time the curse was to be pronounced, the Lord caused Balaam to bless the Israelites and Balaam could not reverse it. Every time he spoke, words of blessing came out of his mouth. Balaam became angry. He wanted King Balak's payoff. His eyes saw more than green. He saw a house full of gold. But he forgot that his God had a heaven filled with gold.

Greed kept eating at him like a cancer. Eventually, he concocted a way to still receive recognition and honor from King Balak. The plan he proposed was an evil plan. It called for the daughters of Moab to seduce the men of Israel. Soon many of Israel's men were crossing the border. They committed whoredom. They even prepared sacrifices and worshipped Baal-peor, the god of the Moabites.

In an act of judgment, the Lord smote Israel with a plague because they defiled themselves by intermarriage with the heathen and committed idolatry. Twenty-four thousand perished. Then Moses was told to gather the army and avenge the children of Israel. In the resulting battle, Balaam was slain. Greed not only benched him, it took his life.

The results of greed are very devastating. Greed is and always has been a killer. It displaces persons by the millions, abandoning them to homelessness and starvation. It forsakes the orphans and the elderly. It leaves beggars to die in the streets. It stops the hands of the church to bless the poor with the necessities they need for living.

We tend to forget that all we see and touch around us belongs to God. He is the rightful owner of everything. We are only stewards responsible for managing what He has provided for us. Haggai, the prophet, reminded the Israelites of this important truth. "The silver is mine, and the gold is mine, says the Lord of hosts." Haggai 2:8.

Since we work for and earn our possessions, it is easy for us to assume ownership. Yet we read in Deuteronomy 8:18, "The Lord gives you power to get wealth."

Greed has its way of distorting our view of ownership. It makes what is God's seem like ours. Furthermore, it instills in us a spirit to hoard what we have accumulated. We become robbers and thieves, blind to the obligations we have to God and others. Like the story that Jesus told about the rich man and Lazareth, we fail or refuse to see Lazareth sitting by our gate. We extend no aid.

The prophet Malachi cried, "Will a man rob God? Yet you have robbed Me. But you say, wherein have we robbed You? In tithes and offerings. You are cursed with a curse: for you have robbed Me." Malachi 3: 8, 9.

The people were blind to the truth that they were robbing God. They refused to recognize what was God's portion and failed to repent of their sin of greed.

Malachi continued, "Bring you all the tithes into the storehouse, that there may be food in My house, and try Me now in this", says the Lord of hosts, "If I will not open for you the windows of heaven, and pour out for you such blessing, that there shall not be room enough to receive it." Malachi 3:10.

Our God challenges us to believe His faithfulness. To put Him to the test. Such generosity generates blessing and joy and peace. The only alternative to a lack of generosity is selfishness and misery. At the end of life our possessions do not follow us. It is far better for us to see afar the shining city of God and go forward in faith, leaving the greed for gain of the present to follow that vision.

I am reminded of a plaque that hung for many years on a wall in my parents' bedroom. It displayed the words, "Only what's done for Christ will last." How true!

Jesus proclaimed, "Do not lay up for yourselves treasures on earth, where moth and rust destroy, and where thieves break in and steal; but lay up for yourselves treasures in heaven, where neither moth nor rust destroys, and where thieves do not break in and steal. For where your treasure is, there your heart will be also." Matthew 6:19-21.

It is of supreme importance that the work of God in the world isn't hindered by lack of funds. Just think what could be accomplished for the kingdom of God if all His people gave Him His portion.

In his book *Called To Maturity*, Myron Augsburger wrote about avarice as a sin of ambition.

> "It is so easy to make an idol out of things, by giving to the pursuit of the material the preeminence that belongs to the pursuit of God. Avarice makes life move around the accumulation of things for one's own pleasure, regardless of its cost to one's spiritual development. In the end it enslaves a man, shriveling the soul, destroying the value of personalities in his thought, and robbing him of peace and pleasure in spiritual and social relations. Pity the man who

has only so-called financial security and no security for eternity. The greater challenges of life are not those which call for physical strength in financial returns, but those which call for moral and spiritual strength in the returns of an endless life."

So in our practice of selfish living, we need to pray, "God, forgive us for sitting on benches of greed."

*SERVE GOD
WITH A LOYAL HEART
AND WITH A WILLING MIND;
FOR THE LORD
SEARCHES ALL HEARTS,
AND UNDERSTANDS
ALL THE INTENT
OF THE THOUGHTS.
IF YOU SEEK HIM,
HE WILL BE FOUND BY YOU.
I CHRONICLES 28:9.*

Wrong Motives

Service to our Lord seldom pours from hearts that are pure in motive. Upon honest examination, we find ourselves performing acts of worship and service for many reasons.

> Others are doing it.
> It's what we have been taught to do and we feel guilty if we don't.
> We are feeding on the praise of others.
> We are being paid for it.
> We want to go to Heaven.

Such motives can cause us to work hard. However, often quite subtly, they trap us into serving God our own way.

> We can be active participants on Sunday in our place of worship, but refrain from being a witness to others of God's love and grace during the week.
> We can make a business of doing God's work.
> We can be prejudiced against some persons while we favor others.
> We can decide to help only those who can do something for us.
> We can give our time to study and teach, but not give of our financial resources.

Serving God *our* way limits the effectiveness of our efforts and can negatively impact persons around us.

During the time of the judges in Israel, before there were kings, there was a man named Micah, who lived on Mount Ephraim. Being wealthy, he set up a house of gods at his estate with images made from silver, then consecrated one of his sons to be his priest. Judges 17.

Later, a priest from the tribe of Levi was on a journey. He stopped at Micah's house for lodging for the night. Micah thought the Lord would bless him if he had a Levite as his priest. He offered the priest lodging, clothing and wages if he would become the priest for his family.

When the priest saw Micah's temple and the silver images, he compromised what he had been taught. Jehovah forbade idol worship. But, the wages were good. He could do well. So he agreed to be the priest for Micah's household. The deal was struck irrespective of the Lord's commands.

Soon afterward, the tribe of Dan sent five men to search for land not claimed by the other tribes of Israel so they could relocate to better territory. On their way, they stopped at Micah's house for food and lodging. Micah's priest took them into the temple and blessed them.

The next morning the five men departed. Eventually, they found unclaimed land that met their expectations. With their mission accomplished, they returned to their tribe.

The children of Dan rejoiced at the news, made preparations to move to the newly discovered location and started out with their herds and cattle. When they were passing by Mount Ephraim, the five scouts recalled the silver images in Micah's temple. They led six hundred armed men to Micah's gate. They raided his temple and took the silver images. When the Levite priest objected, they asked him to join them and become the priest for the tribe of Dan. The priest was delighted with the offer. He went with them.

Micah cried after them, "You have taken away the gods that I made and my priest. What do I have left?" He was forced to retreat empty handed.

The Levite priest in his new position of honor proceeded to serve the Lord in his own way for his own gain. Soon a temple was established and the silver images were set up for the tribe of Dan to worship. The entire tribe of Dan became idolatrous and remained so for six hundred years because of the priest's compromise. They were benched. They were denied the blessing of Jehovah's presence and power among them. They became impoverished. Eventually they were taken away to Assyria as captives, never to return.

When I was young and played softball with the neighborhood teens, our home was the gathering place for the games. There was one fellow my age who didn't enjoy playing sports. Many times he went to the kitchen to help my mother with the dishes instead of joining the game. She never asked him to help, but she did appreciate his efforts. As he dried the dishes, he could watch us play across the street.

My mother gained his confidence. He told her about his home life, his plans for college and his desire to become a minister in his particular denomination. He related that his pastor had advised him to become a minister because it was a lucrative vocation. Concerned that he have a better motive than money, my mother endeavored to help him see that serving the Lord for financial gain was a wrong motive. She explained that we are to serve the Lord according to our calling irrespective of material benefits. Only then do the rewards we receive take on eternal value. In time he did become a minister. And not for the money.

Without a doubt, we can learn something from the examples set by the circuit rider preachers from pioneer days who spent long days on horseback for little or no pay. Only the calling and the opportunity to help others mattered to them. This is the spirit of Christ that we are to exemplify, driven by love to offer ourselves to Christ and others. Such love purifies our motives and keeps the bench at a distance.

LET US NOT BE WEARY IN WELL DOING: FOR IN DUE SEASON WE SHALL REAP IF WE FAINT NOT. GALATIANS 6:9.

Discouragement and Depression

The sudden shifts of life can at times jerk us off course and envelop us in clouds of discouragement and depression. A job offer doesn't materialize. Financial trouble smacks us. A loved one is taken away. Life goes wrong. The difficulties in which we become submerged can effectively reduce our momentum to move forward in God's work. We become drained and incapacitated. There is little energy to be and do for others. We can barely care for ourselves. We lose motivation and purpose. So we withdraw from the action of the game and struggle toward the bench. We find ourselves in need of ministering, and unable to minister to others.

Loneliness can close in upon us. We may feel physically isolated or emotionally abandoned and spiritually alone. This situation may have precipitated from childhood experiences where parents were too busy or apathetic and were too absent. Rejection and abuse may have ingrained feelings of not being important and needed, and not being loved. But our God doesn't want us to be lonely. He created us for His pleasure and has made us creatures of worth. He cherishes fellowship with us and wants us to be in His presence. He realizes that loneliness and depression block our potential to do the work He has planned for us.

The greatest of persons among us can at times become crushed under discouraging circumstances. The Prophet Elijah longed for an opportunity to demonstrate the power of God to the idolatrous people of Israel. God's people had been lured into the worship of Baal. King Ahab of Israel had built a temple for the worship of Baal in Samaria and the people had forsaken worship of Jehovah, the Lord. Because of Ahab's sin, God sent three years of drought to Israel. Finally, Elijah met with King Ahab. The king wanted rain. Elijah challenged the king to gather the four hundred and fifty prophets of Baal and all the children of Israel on Mount Carmel to prove that the idol Baal had the power to send rain. I Kings 18.

What a day it was! The prophets cried to their god Baal to bring fire down from heaven and light the altar they had built for sacrifice. They chanted and cut themselves, but no fire came. Finally, Elijah announced that it was his turn to call upon the true God of Heaven to light the altar with fire. He summoned men to fetch twelve barrels of water and pour it over the altar of sacrifice. Then, in response to his simple prayer to Jehovah, fire descended from heaven and the altar burst into flame. Even the stones of the altar were consumed. The false prophets of Baal were promptly slain. Then God sent rain. But the children of Israel remained unchanged in heart. They still continued their idolatrous worship to Baal.

Ahab told the wicked queen Jezebel what Elijah had done. She swiftly announced that Elijah would be killed. Elijah fled into the wilderness to hide. Deeply discouraged, he prayed to die. He had expected the children of Israel to worship the true God after they witnessed the fire consuming the altar and the coming of rain. Instead, he had to flee for his life. Elijah fell asleep under a juniper tree. When he awoke, an angel of God provided him with food and water. Even this didn't take his depression away. Then Elijah traveled on to Mount Horeb and found a cave in which to stay. After forty days of sulking in self-pity and depression, Elijah heard the voice of God.

God simply asked, "Elijah, what are you doing here?" Elijah replied that the children of Israel had forsaken the Lord, killed his prophets, and he was the only one left who had remained faithful to God. He had done his best and it hadn't made a difference.

The Lord informed Elijah that there were seven thousand in Israel who had not bowed their knee to Baal. He was not alone as he had thought. Elijah was instructed to get off the bench. He was told to anoint kings! Elijah was excited about this news and returned to anoint Hazael as king over Syria and Jehu as king over Israel.

It is not uncommon for the children of God to experience burnout. Discouragement from the failure to achieve the results we expect robs our energy. In our haste to climb the ladder and strive for perfection, even while performing good deeds, exhaustion and bitterness can overtake us. Our service to God can be reduced to mechanical, mundane and meaningless acts. We become trapped by depression. We feel useless.

The enemy of our souls seeks to attack us through the daily circumstances of our lives. He attacks our bodies through sickness and disease. He attacks us through troubles within our families that cause communications to break down, that breed unforgiveness, bitterness and strife. He attacks us on the job by creating misunderstandings and friction between fellow co-workers. He attacks us through unexpected financial problems or the loss of a job.

These attacks can entrap us in a cycle of defeat that incorporates stress, fear, worry, doubt, weariness, discouragement and depression. It is easily recognized that many of us as God's people today are victims of stress. Our minds and bodies can become weakened and we can lose the ability to cope. Our minds can become bombarded with fear, worry and doubt. Faith can no longer be released. We find ourselves sitting on the bench. We need to seek a touch from God to heal our faith and revitalize our spirits.

In the book *Healing Life's Hurts*, Ron Lee Davis wrote about a striking observation he realized in regard to the root of discouragement.

> "I've noticed a tendency which I believe may be at the root of much of our discouragement: We sense that God is calling us to some new adventure, and then we decide how we're going to get there, how long it's going to take, and what route we're going to travel. But somewhere along the way, it dawns on us that God's timetable doesn't coincide with ours. His schedule for us includes some layovers, some setbacks, some storms, some things we never anticipated. The inevitable result is discouragement.
>
> When we find ourselves powerless to alter our circumstances, we're going to have to alter our response to those circumstances - and that means we're going to have to find God's perspective for our discouragement."

An article written by Nate Adams for *Decision Magazine* addressed the subject of waking up feeling discouraged. He recommended three steps to take when we feel that way:

1. *Welcome back faith*. Pinpoint the reason for your feelings. Then apply the Bible to your circumstances. For example, "I have the strength to face all conditions by the power that Christ gives me."

2. *Wecome back hope*. Find something to look forward to. It may be something small - a trip to an ice cream shop or a telephone call to a friend. Cultivate a mindset

169

of hope that is based on God's promises. The Scriptures assure us that God has an investment in us, so he wants hope to remain in us.

3. ***Welcome back love.*** Demonstrate love to God and to the people around you. The Bible urges us to love one another. As you focus on actions of love toward God (worship, prayer, singing, even crying) and toward the people around you (encouraging, giving, helping), you will escape the traps of inward focus and self-pity. The circumstances that caused you to wake up blue may start to become less important, and the things that God says should remain - faith, hope, love - will become more important.

There is also a time to rest. Jesus recognized the need for rest and practiced it. We read in the Bible that He frequently went away by Himself to a quiet place where He found peace of soul and refreshment of spirit in the presence of His Father. As we enter into this rest, a whole new way of living can open up to us. God knows our times of struggle and longs to pour encouragement and hope into our lives. There is never a time when we are abandoned by Him. We simply need to schedule some appointments with Him.

The way back from the bench to the game requires a readjustment of our vision. Our eyes need to be lifted from viewing the magnitude of our needs to seeing the greatness of our God. It is the realization of God's promises and His abilities that brings the miracles we desire. No circumstance or trial or persecution that enters our lives has the ultimate power to conquer and defeat us. The power we receive through our Lord is greater than all. With every hardship that we face comes the provision for total victory. God uses our difficulties to perfect and strengthen us. His purpose is to work good for us. His design is to make us successful players in the game of life. In the valleys of our lives, He is tuning our voices, and in the night, He is preparing us for singing.

YOUR WORDS WERE FOUND,
AND I ATE THEM,
AND YOUR WORD WAS TO ME
THE JOY AND REJOICING
OF MY HEART.
JEREMIAH 15:16.

Frank H Leaman

Malnourishment

For many years I directed Junior Church programs for several different churches. During that time I told hundreds of children's stories, most of which were based on actual occurrences. One time I wanted to convey the meaning of being malnourished, and I thought of telling a story about a squirrel. It is written here as a fable.

Once upon a time there was a squirrel named Sam. He had all the food he could eat right in his house that was located at a choice spot in a huge walnut tree. And he loved walnuts! All he had to do to get walnuts was go out on a nearby limb or skip down the tree trunk to get walnuts that had fallen to the ground under his magnificent tree.

Sam was a handsome squirrel. He had a beautiful, big bushy tail. He was young, quick and alert. He also was quite strong. But he wasn't like the other squirrels that lived around him. They believed in eating a balanced diet and ate a large variety of nuts. They ran all over the woods seeking different kinds of nuts to eat so their bodies would be fed all of the vitamins and minerals they needed to develop properly. Sam only ate walnuts. He thought other kinds of nuts were disgusting. The other squirrels kept telling Sam that he should eat many different kinds of nuts like they were eating.

"Hogwash," Sam would retort. "There's no need to do that. I'm as healthy as all of you are. And I'm strong too. And look at my bushy tail. See how pretty it is. That's because I'm not always getting twigs and leaves tangled in it like all of you when you scamper through the woods like idiots looking for strange nuts."

But, indeed, Sam wasn't as healthy as he thought. Gradually, his bones began to get brittle. His hair began to get coarse. His muscles got sore and stiff. He wasn't getting much exercise as he sat in his walnut tree and watched the other squirrels scamper about. His body was wearing out before it should. But he was stubborn. He pretended to be strong and healthy. He refused to eat anything but walnuts. He began to get colds, headaches and coughing spells. When he had to cough, he would stay inside his tree house so the other squirrels couldn't hear him. The other squirrels still had a lot of energy to play, but Sam needed more and more sleep.

Finally, the walnut tree squirrel got very sick. The other squirrels searched diligently to find choice nuts to help Sam get better. They quickly brought the nuts to Sam to eat.

Sam did try to taste some of them, but he didn't like them and he spit them out. He hadn't learned to enjoy these tastes when he was young.

Several days later the walnut tree squirrel died. The other squirrels buried him under his walnut tree. Then they erected a tombstone at his grave with the words, "Here lies Stubborn Sam, the walnut tree squirrel, who died from malnutrition before his time because he refused to eat a balanced diet."

A surprising number of God's people suffer from spiritual malnutrition and are plightfully malnourished. Even when the resources for spiritual health are all around them. They fail to assimilate God's word, the bread of life. They neglect to clothe themselves with the righteousness of Christ and the whole armor of God. They refuse to exercise offensive and defensive activities in warfare against the enemy of their souls. Out of shape. Weak. Faint. Bleeding.

The Apostle Paul wrote to the Christians at Corinth, "Many are weak and sickly among you and many sleep." I Corinthians 11:30.

Also, in the Old Testament, God warned His people Israel to avoid neglect and decisions that would lead to their impoverishment.

"Take heed to yourselves, lest you forget the covenant of the Lord your God, which He made with you. You shall love the Lord your God with all your heart, with all your soul, and with all your strength. And these words, which I command you today, shall be in your heart; you shall teach them diligently unto your children, and shall talk of them when you sit in your house, and when you walk by the way, and when you lie down, and when you rise up. You shall bind them as a sign on your hand, and they shall be as frontlets between your eyes. You shall write them on the posts of your house, and on your gates. So shall it be, when the Lord your God brings you into the land of which he swore unto your fathers, to Abraham, Isaac, and Jacob, to give you large and beautiful cities, which you did not build, houses full of all good things, which you did not fill, hewn-out wells, which you did not dig, vineyards and olive trees which you did not plant - when you have eaten and are full - then beware lest you forget the Lord who brought you out of the land of Egypt, from the house of bondage. You shall fear the Lord your God, and serve Him. Deuteronomy 4:23; 6:5-13.

These verses very graphically illustrate the necessity for God's people to devotedly and persistently remember the words of God. But before we can remember them, we need to learn them. God has spoken. His word is our source of growth. We have the responsibility to study. To hear. To listen.

Throughout the Bible we are continually instructed to hear the word of the Lord. Jesus cried out again and again, "He who has ears to hear, let him hear." Luke 14:35.

The Apostle Peter wrote to the scattered Jewish believers, "As newborn babes, desire the pure milk of the word, that you may grow thereby." I Peter 2:2.

And the Apostle Paul admonished Timothy, "Study to show yourself approved unto God, a workman that need not be ashamed, rightly dividing the word of truth." II Timothy 2:15.

The Bible gives tremendous credibility to the words of God. Jesus said, "Heaven and earth shall pass away, but My words shall not pass away." Matthew 24:35.

The Psalmist wrote, "The words of the Lord are pure words: like silver tried in a furnace of earth, purified seven times. You shall keep them, O Lord, you shall preserve them from this generation forever." Psalm 12:6, 7.

So the words of God alone of all words endure forever. These are the words of pure truth. These are the words that show us what God is like. These are the words of everlasting life.

David wrote volumes in the Psalms about the benefits of knowing God's word. Note the following references taken from Psalm 119.

> God's word is our hope (vs. 49, 114).
> God's word gives us understanding (vs. 34, 104, 169).
> God's word strengthens us (v. 28).
> God's word quickens us (vs. 25, 93).
> God's word is delightful (vs. 16, 162).
> God's word leads us to reverence God (v. 38).
> God's word comforts us (vs. 50, 76).
> God's word cleanses us (vs. 9).
> God's word keeps us from defiling ourselves (vs. 1, 11, 101).
> God's word reveals His mercy and salvation (v. 41).
> God's word gives life (v. 116).
> God's word gives light (v. 130).
> God's word directs our steps (v. 133).
> God's word is our source of truth (v. 142).
> God's word gives us awareness of righteousness (v. 172).

In spite of God's warnings to Israel that His words should not be forgotten, the people forgot them. The desire for God's words was quenched by neglect, by looking over the fence to observe what the heathen were doing and by inviting fires of passion to ignite.

Finally, the Lord called Amos, a herdsman, to prophesy to the house of Jacob concerning the plight that a forgetful people had brought upon themselves. Amos cried God's verdict to the people.

> "Behold the days come, says the Lord God, that I will send
> a famine in the land, not a famine of bread, nor a thirst for

water, but of hearing the words of the Lord: And they shall wander from sea to sea, and from the north even to the east, they shall run to and fro to seek the word of the Lord, and shall not find it." Amos 8:11, 12.

Just like a refused gift. The words of God were taken away. And so was the remnant that survived the armies of conquest. They were carried into captivity. In the land of Babylon, the hardness of the bench birthed within the captives a desire to feed again on the saving words of their God. In repentance and sincere seeking, they were once again led by God to the Promised Land.

Frank H Leaman

WHO AMONG YOU
FEARS THE LORD?
WHO OBEYS THE VOICE
OF HIS SERVANT?
WHO WALKS IN DARKNESS
AND HAS NO LIGHT?
LET HIM TRUST
IN THE NAME OF THE LORD
AND RELY UPON HIS GOD.
ISAIAH 50:10.

Frank H Leaman

Misplaced Trust

We have all experienced times when our faith didn't bring about what we had hoped it would accomplish. In these circumstances, our faith was dealt a blow. But a closer examination of the situation may reveal that we had trusted in the wrong thing.

Our ministry to God rapidly becomes anemic and ineffective from a misplaced trust. While faith in God can move mountains, faith in someone or something other than God leads to disastrous results. Cult leaders like Jim Jones, who founded the People's Temple, and David Koresh, a self-declared Messiah who headed the Branch Davidian Compound at Waco, Texas, led their devoted followers into emotional havoc, suicide and death.

We, as God's people, are warned in the scriptures to flee proclaimers of false doctrines. Spiritual energy can quickly be drained from us when we trust in anything other than God. We can exhibit the greatest faith, but if that faith isn't in the Almighty God, it is a faith that cannot save us.

The Prophet Samuel wrote about a time when the children of Israel put their faith in an object rather than God. I Samuel 4. The Israelites had become morally corrupt. They no longer had favor with God and deliverance from their enemies. The Philistines and Israel were at war. In a battle at Aphek, Israel lost four thousand men. They retreated to their camp at Ebenezer. There, the elders of Israel developed a plan which everyone thought was brilliant. They advised getting the *Ark of the Covenant* of the Lord from the tabernacle in Shiloh so they could carry it into battle and be victorious. The Ark, a wooden chest designed to hold the stone tablets on which the commandments of God were written by His own hand, signified God's presence among His people.

When the *Ark of the Covenant* arrived in the camp of Israel, all the people shouted. The enemy heard their joyous celebrating. When the Philistines learned what was happening, they became terrified. But their fear became an asset. They vowed to fight like wild men. In the battle that ensued, Israel suffered a great slaughter. They fled to their tents. Worse yet, the *Ark of the Covenant* was captured by the Philistines.

181

How could a people celebrating such great faith fail so miserably? They became the victims of misplaced trust. Their trust was supposed to be fixed on Jehovah, not on a box of wood. For Israel, it was easier to trust in a plan to achieve victory that displayed a symbol of their faith than it was to address the need to confess their sins. Their spiritual condition was not conducive to God's blessings upon them. They had four strikes against them.

They were morally impoverished.
They had committed rampant idolatry.
Their priests were profane.
They lacked a genuine love for God.

The children of Israel trusted in a substitute for God that made no demands. That required no change. That could not save. That produced no spiritual growth.

Today, it is often easier for us to trust in baptism, faithful church attendance, good deeds, our own specially concocted philosophies of life, or the avoidance of committing major sins, than it is to recognize and own our sins, make our confession, and trust ourselves to God's forgiveness and keeping. False hope yields catastrophic consequences. It is a hope that is not fortified by obedience to God and genuine love for Him. It is a faith driven by what we desire rather than by what God has designed for us. False hope weakens our ministry and benches us. It sets stages of confusion and emptiness, causing us to lose our way.

When my mother was attending college, one of her friends had a problem related to misplaced trust. The young woman was a dedicated Christian. She earnestly desired to pursue the will of God for her life. This included seeking the mind of God in regard to whom she would marry.

The woman became particularly attracted to a young man and hoped that he would begin a relationship with her. One night she had a dream that greatly excited her. In the framework of her dream she saw a huge map of Africa. Most of the continent was black, but in a certain white area she saw her name. Then the name of the young man appeared under her name. She assumed from the dream that God was revealing to her that she would marry this man she desired, and they would serve the Lord as missionaries in Africa.

In her excitement, she shared her dream with some of her best friends, desiring their counsel and prayers. She felt certain that her interpretation of her dream was correct.

After a considerable period of time, the young man she liked failed to show any interest in her. Finally, unable to control herself any longer, she approached him and told him about her dream and her feelings for him. He was stunned. He told her that he had no feelings for her whatsoever, and he certainly didn't feel a call to serve the Lord as a missionary in Africa.

She was crushed and bewildered. Feeling like a fool. In her confusion she sought counseling. She learned that it is not advisable to put one's confidence solely in dreams. She recognized that quite subtly her own desires had been substituted for the Lord's will for her life. In time she received knowledge of her calling in life, married another and found happiness.

We are masters at self-deception. Often we reason illogically. Self gets in the way and crowds out communication from God. In our pursuits to satisfy our desires we can easily arrive at a place where we give our worship to vain identities.

The most deplorable, ungodly king in the history of Judah was King Ahaz. Surprisingly, he was the child of a godly heritage. His father, King Jotham, his grandfather, King Uzziah, his great grandfather, King Amaziah, and his great great grandfather, King Joash, all brought revival in Judah and encouraged the worship of Jehovah. God blessed their reigns with prosperity and gave them victory over their enemies. But such blessings were denied King Ahaz. II Chronicles 28.

King Ahaz began his reign by making molten images for his subjects to worship. He burned his children in fire sacrifices like the heathen whom the Lord had cast out before the children of Israel. He burned incense before his idols and led the people into gross idolatry.

So the Lord raised up the king of Syria to defeat the army of Judah. The Syrians carried a great number into captivity. Also, the king of Israel invaded Judah from the north and slew one hundred twenty thousand more valiant men in a single day. The Lord punished the people of Judah because of their transgressions.

But the severe punishment and impoverishment of the Lord didn't bring King Ahaz to repentance. Rather, in his stubbornness and blindness, he reasoned that since he had been defeated by the king of

Syria, the gods of the Syrians were stronger than Jehovah, so he began sacrificing to the gods of Damascus so they would help him also. In rejection of Jehovah, he cut the sacred vessels of the house of the Lord in pieces and shut the doors of the temple in Jerusalem. Then he proceeded to set up altars to worship false gods in every city of Judah.

The Lord moved to terminate his reign. King Ahaz died a premature death at the age of thirty-six. The people denied him burial in the sepulchers of the kings of Israel. Such was the price of his misplaced trust. No miracles. No deliverance. No peace. Gods of stone hear not, see not and help not.

There was a group of Jews in Jesus' time that claimed to have great faith in God. They thought that they were God's most favored. They were the children of Abraham, and they believed that they were faithfully doing the work of God. After all, they had the duty to keep the defiled, the sinners and the unclean out of the synagogues. They were the guardians and keepers of the law. In their opinion, they were at the top of the spiritual ladder.

But Jesus had a much different opinion about them and He told them so. He said that their faith in God was actually a faith based on keeping the laws of the religious order that they had established. He reminded them that they frequently took the liberty to disobey these laws themselves while making everyone else follow them. They were worshipping themselves and their religious order. They were proud, gloating in their accomplishments and seeking the praise of the people. Jesus said that they played favorites and oppressed the poor. They were self-righteous. They declared themselves to be holy, but were steeped in unholiness.

Jesus pronounced judgment upon them because they were spiritually blind and were without mercy. He said that inside they were full of extortion, lies and sin. They wanted everyone to think that they were righteous, but they were filled with iniquity. So what was their warped faith in God doing for them? Absolutely nothing! It is significant to recall that it was this group of religious leaders who had Jesus put to death, thus committing the greatest crime of all time. To them, their faith said that they were doing the right thing with Jesus, but nothing could have been further from the truth.

When it comes to the assessment of our faith in God, we can easily deceive ourselves and totally miss the mark just as the Pharisees did. There are a number of reasons for this.

An unwillingness to acknowledge our sins.
An ignorance of what the Bible teaches about God.
A refusal to believe that we need God's help and salvation.
An arrogance that places our beliefs and philosophies above God and His word.

It is easy for us at times to trust in something or someone other than God because we forget who God really is or don't take the time to find out who He is.

It is crucial that we realize the greatness of our God in whom we trust. Our God is astronomically awesome. We know Him as the Creator and Sustainer of the heavens and the earth and all life forms. Is He a trillion times greater than us? Most probably much more. Ponder the vast domain God controls.

The Hubble telescope in its orbit 380 miles above the earth has the optical capability to view the light of a single firefly 10,000 miles away. It recently photographed a black hole fifty million light years away. The force of gravity around black holes is so great that even light cannot escape. The concentration of matter in this black hole is so dense that it's weight is calculated to be equal to two billion three hundred million suns.

On February 23, 1987, the explosion of Supernova 1987A was seen by an astronomer in Chile without magnification. The blast was so powerful that it released as much energy in a single second as our sun will release in ten billion years. This explosion actually occurred one hundred seventy thousand years ago. The light from the explosion traveling at six trillion miles each year took that long to reach our earth.

But our God does not limit His attention to the big things. The tiny things in His creation totally boggle our imagination also. He uses building blocks for His universe that are incredibly small. Atoms. Electrons. Subatomic particles. His creation around us has innumerable miniature aspects. Single-celled life forms. Microscopic plants that bloom beautiful flowers. He created man from dust and breathed life into him. Immediately trillions of diverse cells came alive and began functioning in harmony with God's design. Blood began to flow through twelve thousand miles of arteries, veins, and capillaries to supply nutrients and oxygen to every cell, organ and tissue in the body, pumped by an organ that would beat over two billion times in a normal lifetime of seventy-two years. Some capillaries were so small that only a single blood cell could pass through them at a time. The brain, comprised of ten billion nerve cells, began it's countless calculations from minute electrical pulses received from the sensing organs. Two million calculations for each second of vision to reveal size, color, depth and a sense of motion. A body, whole and functioning, with chemical reactions so complex that it staggers our ability to discover them. Every living minute cell in the human body contains a spiral of DNA molecules five feet long that bears the genetic code that makes us unique individuals.

Our God is a God to be trusted and worshipped. He cares for us so much that Jesus said, "The very hairs of your head are all numbered," Matthew 10:30. He reminded His disciples that God takes care of the sparrows, and He certainly will take care of His followers because they are much more valuable than sparrows.

The Apostle John wrote of a time in our future when the God of the universe will receive the praise He deserves.

> "And every creature which is in heaven, and on the earth, and under the earth, and such as are in the sea, and all that are in them, heard I saying, Blessing, and honor, and glory, and power, be unto Him who sits on the throne, and to the Lamb, forever and ever!" Revelation 5:13.

In his book *Born Crucified*, L.E. Maxwell wrote about the testimony of J. Hudson Taylor, the founder of the China Inland Mission, in regard to overcoming anxiety.

> After several months of agony and struggle to realize more life, holiness and power in his soul, he came in final and utter self-despair to rest upon the Faithful One. In a letter to his sister he wrote, "The sweetest part is the rest which full identification with Christ brings. I am no longer anxious about anything, for He, I know, is able to carry out His will and His will is mine. It makes no matter where He

places me or how. That is rather for Him to consider than for me; for the easiest positions He must give me grace, and in the most difficult, His grace is sufficient. So, if God place me in great perplexity, must He not give me much guidance; in positions of great difficulty, much grace; in circumstances of great pressure and trial, much strength? As to work, mine was never so plentiful, so responsible, or so difficult; but the weight and strain are all gone. His resources are mine, for He is mine."

How beneficial it is for us to trust God now! It keeps us in the game.

A HAUGHTY SPIRIT INVITES A FALL. PROVERBS 16:18

Frank H Leaman

OVERCONFIDENCE

Overconfidence is defined as the tendency to be more confident than correct or to overestimate the accuracy of one's beliefs. We may feel overconfident about facts or how we will act for the present moment or in our future. This degree of confidence does not necessarily lead to wise or correct actions. It may well entail overestimating abilities and judgments, and lead us to disregard instruction we have been given and good common sense. At times, we may feel like we can do things with our eyes shut, but often danger lurks ahead. Danger that has the power to bench us.

I remember riding my bike during my boyhood days, thinking it was great to go down the road with my arms folded across my chest. I took pride in my ability to keep my balance and dared to ride faster and faster this way. But one time while I was looking to the left hoping to impress someone, my front tire hit a stone. In a moment the front wheel turned sharply and I was thrown forward over the handlebars. Needless to say, my landing was painful. My hands, elbows and knees were cut open. Some dirt and fine stones became lodged in some of my wounds which were later scrubbed away by my mother. The iodine really stung! Through this experience I learned that overconfidence has a price tag attached.

It is quite easy for us as believers to become overconfident about our spiritual strength. This attitude makes us vulnerable to the onslaught of evil forces. The enemy of our souls takes every advantage possible when we let our guard down and fail to stay alert. Obviously, this is why Paul advised the Corinthian believers to "Be watchful, stand firm in your faith, be courageous, be strong" (1 Cor. 16:13). We stand against the devil, not by our own strength and wisdom, but in the name and power of Jesus, the Christ.

Peter, a disciple of Jesus, had a problem of being overconfident. He had a high opinion of himself and was rather cocky. He was a rough, short-fused fisherman who was loud and impulsive and often acted without thinking first. Neil Anderson in his book, *Victory Over the Darkness*, describes Peter as the John Wayne of the New Testament - a real door slammer, who had no problem telling anyone what was on his mind or how he felt. Neil referred to him as the one-legged apostle because he always had one foot in his mouth. One

191

minute he made the greatest confession of all time that Jesus was the Christ, the promised Messiah, and a few minutes later he tried to tell Jesus that He had it all wrong about being killed by the priests and scribes. He couldn't see such a death for Jesus in the picture.

It was Peter who promised to follow Jesus anywhere, even to the death, saying that he would never deny Him. However, only a few hours later in the courtyard at Jesus' trial, to save his own skin, he cursed and swore that he didn't know Jesus. At least Peter was closer to Jesus at that moment than the other disciples who had fled in terror, but he wasn't willing to be identified with Jesus and be sentenced with Him. Fierce and tough as he was, he wasn't willing to stand by the side of Jesus and take the brutal treatment Jesus was receiving. So, three times he denied that he knew Jesus. Then the cock crowed, and Peter remembered that, only a few hours earlier, he had promised Jesus that he would never deny Him. Peter experienced his darkest hour and his blackest night. The cutting truth that he had deserted and denied his Lord, the truth that he was nothing more than a big coward ate away at his heart, and he went out and wept bitterly.

The trap we often set for ourselves is one of failure to rely upon God for help. We depend on our own efforts. An essential ingredient in service to God is the guidance and power of the Holy Spirit. There is a real danger in being overconfident, because it leads to carelessness and irresponsibility.

This truth brings to mind a story my aunt and uncle told me about an experience they had while serving as missionaries in Haiti. My aunt drove a jeep to bring students to her Bible classes and to do visitation. In that culture, it was believed that a woman could not possibly have the skills to drive a vehicle. When the people saw her coming, they ran from the road in fear!

After a number of trips in the jeep, the students began to think that it was easy to drive a vehicle. It was just a matter of pushing pedals and turning the steering wheel. Then a student named Abraham told the others, "She is a great teacher, but I can drive this jeep better than she can."

Now, all of the students had been strictly forbidden to start or drive any vehicle. But, one day when my uncle was unloading stone with some of the students, he heard the jeep engine roar. He turned and saw Abraham in the driver's seat. The jeep was in reverse and the throttle pedal was against the floor boards. Stones and dirt were flying as the jeep wheels bounced up and down. The jeep climbed a pile of rocks. The drive wheels extended over the pile and were spinning at full speed. Abraham was in shock! My uncle ran to the jeep and turned off the engine. Had the jeep gone futher, it would have tumbled down a thirty foot embankment. Abraham could have been injured or even killed.

Abraham did not understand his limitations. Overconfidence gave him false self-confidence. He tried to do something he was very unprepared to do.

Like Peter and Abraham, at times we fail to recognize our limitations and become overconfident. Instead, we should look to God for direction, wisdom and strength. He will help us play our best in the game.

Frank H Leaman

NOW MAY OUR LORD
JESUS CHRIST HIMSELF,
AND OUR GOD AND FATHER,
WHO HAS LOVED US,
AND GIVEN US
EVERLASTING CONSOLATION
AND GOOD HOPE BY GRACE,
COMFORT YOUR HEARTS,
AND ESTABLISH YOU
IN EVERY GOOD
WORD AND WORK.
II THESSALONIANS 2:16, 17.

Frank H Leaman

Bereavement and Personal Tragedy

There are times in life's experiences when tragedy strikes with sudden cruelty. Like an avalanche, it can sweep away a lover, a parent, a child or a cherished friend. Accidents can maim and cripple us. Disease can pull us tenaciously toward the brink of death. We become paralyzed by hurt. Haunted by darkness of night that refuses to break into day. Broken. Suffering. Sometimes fearful. Sometimes angry. Longing for answers to our questions. Trauma moves deeply within our souls and takes a bitter toll.

These are times of benching; often undeserved and unexpected. The pain of bereavement, the fear, the anger and the agony of not knowing why, force us into isolation and aloneness. The benching can be brief or it can be long. Sometimes it can become permanent. In the horror of trauma, we can either groan for a glimpse of God's face or we can moan in bitterness and rebellion. When we fail to let go of the pain and hurt, bitterness and an inability to forgive can overcome us and drive us into depression and despair. Our entire lives can become distorted by holding onto pain. We tend to think others don't care.

Who wants to see our crying eyes?
Who wants to hear our penetrating questions?
Who wants to feel our pain?
Who wants to hear our complaints?
Who wants to share our bitterness?

But, when we hurt the worst, we need the body of Christ the most. We need to recognize the kind of God we serve.

We have a God who cares about what happens to us.
We have a God who understands.
We have a God who loves us with an infinite love.
We have a God who grieves with us.
We have a God who has promised to bring good from every unfortunate circumstance that affects our living.
We have a God who provides victory and peace even for the dying.

197

Our Heavenly Father is the source of hope and comfort. He is the answer to our aloneness. Seeking the mind of God and yielding to His enablement lifts us from our deserts and valleys to the mountaintops. There are those among us who would readily testify that their marks of tragedy, their losses and their crosses have enabled them to serve the Lord more fully than would have been possible otherwise. This often proves true for God's children who have been hurt the most and who ultimately become the most caring and loving.

When Absolom, King David's son, stormed the city of Jerusalem with his followers, David was forced to flee the palace to save his life. We are given a glimpse of David's torn heart in Psalm 3 during the calamitous hours that followed.

He cried to the heavens, "Lord, how are they increased that trouble me? Many are they that rise up against me."

Then, David's focus shifted from the betrayal by his son and the multitudes aligned against him to the incredible resources in God's storehouse, and he continued, "But you, O Lord, are a shield for me, My glory and the One who lifts up my head."

In our worst experiences, God in His mercy reaches from His throne room, desiring to lift our heads. He wants us to know that He is Sovereign. That we will never completely understand the reasons for our plight until we stroll with Him in glory. He wants us to recognize that He is still our hope, our provider, our shield, our strong tower. That He knows our pain. That He hurts with us. That His supply of love, mercy and grace is inexhaustible. That His storehouse of provision for us is always full. That He will surely bless our continued trust in Him as our Savior and Lord.

When the judges ruled in Israel, a famine impoverished the land. Elimelech with his wife, Naomi, and their two sons relocated to the land of Moab to find relief from the drought. Ruth 1. During the ten years they lived in Moab, the sons married women of Moab. Then tragedy struck. The untimely deaths of Elimelech and his sons left Naomi alone and stricken with grief. She told her daughters-in-law, Ruth and Orpah, that the hand of God had moved against her. They wept together. Then Naomi announced that she was going to return to her homeland. Orpah chose to stay with her parents in Moab, but Ruth insisted on accompanying Naomi to live with her.

As Naomi and Ruth crossed the border into Judah, can't you feel the gnawing sorrow of Naomi's heart? The depression? The loneliness? The hurt? A husband who would never hold her again. No sons to pride in and enjoy. No grandchildren to cuddle and love. Coming home empty. Nothing to look forward to but poverty. How painful it must have been! Each thought piercing her heart like a dagger.

But God had a wonderful plan for her. A task undreamed of for her to delight in. A kinsman fell in love with Ruth and married her. Soon they had a son. As the darling baby boy was placed in Naomi's arms, the neighbor women said, "Oh, Naomi, blessed be the Lord who has provided you with a kinsman who is to you a restorer of life." Ruth 4:14.

Naomi took the child and held it against her bosom. Her heart was rejoicing. She became the nurse for the child. What wonderful times they must have had together! The child's name was Obed, the father of Jesse, the father of King David.

Leonard Bolton, Assemblies of God missionary to the Lisu tribespeople, lost his first wife and newborn son during childbirth soon after they had arrived in China. In his book *China Call*, he wrote about that painful experience.

"All that day I lay on my bed unable to move; the suffering of my heart overwhelmed me. Why has God done this? Why did He call me to China only to lose my wife, the darling of my heart? These and a thousand other questions burned in my head. I felt numb, floating around in a consciousless void. Several China Inland Mission missionaries gathered around me and prayed, but I seemed beyond the reach of God or man.

Because there was no way to embalm bodies, missionary friends held the funeral the next day for both mother and son in the China Inland Mission Church. Outside the walled city was a foreign cemetery surrounded by an iron fence for keeping out wild animals. In a daze, I found myself taken out of the city in a ricksha to this cemetery. When the coffin was lowered, I wanted to throw myself into that gaping hole and bury myself with my wife and child.

Several days went by. I was still in a daze. Then one morning, I rose from my bed and slipped away for a walk. I came to the city wall and climbed up the steps on its inward embankment, then walked the well-worn path along the top that went around the city. I looked at the curved tile roofs of the houses on one side and the rice paddies with the lake and mountains in the distance on the other side. The beauty of the scenery moved me somewhat, and I felt a little lifted in spirit by the sunshine. I walked on and on.

As evening shadows began to fall, gloom once more settled over me. I stopped and looked over the outer edge of the wall with its sheer drop of over fifty feet. Suddenly, the enemy seemed to whisper to me, 'Why don't you just end it all? It's not worth the sacrifice! Throw yourself down from the wall and end all your misery.'

Looking over the edge, I noticed the vines and wild flowers hanging precariously from the stones. Then, as I stepped closer, another voice clearly spoke: 'I gave My Beloved for you. Can you not give your beloved for Me?'

I broke before the Lord. His promises poured into my aching heart like soothing oil: 'I will never leave thee nor forsake thee ... Have I not promised? Be strong and of good courage! ... Rise up and possess the land!'

A stream of comfort and courage began to rise up from deep within my being until it became like a rushing river. I sat down on a large stone and wept like a baby, with healing tears of release. 'Thank you, Lord! Thank you for bringing me to my senses. You are worthy of any sacrifice. I will trust You to help me. You will never leave me nor forsake me!'

As I began to praise the Lord, a miracle took place in my heart. New strength flowed into my soul. I felt like a new man. The power of God surged over me like a mighty torrent. I began praising the Lord and speaking in another language given to me by the Holy Spirit. My spirit experienced release and victory."

This is the secret to leaving the benches our tragic experiences thrust us upon. This is the way to get back in the game. Thanking our God and praising His name in the midst of our tragedy, realizing that there is a road yet to be traveled. That new heights await us.

Several years ago one of my cousins was killed in a head-on collision. Another vehicle driven by a drunken driver crossed into his lane of traffic early one morning as he was on his way to work. The tragedy seemed so unfair.

At his funeral as I was expressing my sorrow to his mother, I said, "I keep wondering why this happened. Jim just rededicated his life to the Lord. I don't understand why his life was taken so prematurely."

I'll never forget her answer. She looked at me rather serenely and replied, "Ours is not to question why, neither do we need to know." The trust my aunt possessed in God was like a rock. Unshakable. Was she grieving? Certainly she was. Did the sudden loss hurt? Indeed it did. Like a knife driven deeply into the soul. But she comforted herself in the Lord. She rested in the solace of His sovereignty. She knew her son was with God.

I have often pondered the miracle of her faith statement. I've come to the conclusion that the escape from times of catastrophic bereavement is possible along the avenue of total surrender of the situation to God. Believing.

> Believing that God knows.
> Believing that God cares.
> Believing that God is grieving also.
> Believing that God is able to do as He promised and create good from bad.

Perhaps we learn our greatest lessons when our sorrow is the deepest and our pain is the most intense. But we need to seek the answers to the right questions. In times of tragedy, we should not ask "why," but "what." What are we to learn? What are we to gain? What are we to do next? Storms of suffering have the potential to grow our faith as we look forward and not backward, asking "what", not "why".

Hear Job's awesome statement of faith in the midst of his excruciating suffering, "I know that my Redeemer lives." Job 19:25. It was Job's rock-like faith that turned his losses into gains. That search that cried out for a confrontation with God that eventually focused the Almighty God in his vision so that he could declare in reverence and triumph, "Now my eyes have seen You." Job 42:5 NIV.

The key to bearing our suffering is couched in recognizing the greatness and sovereignty of our God. Feeling His presence. Being encompassed with His love. Learning that He is our El-Shaddai, our All Sufficient One. Casting ourselves upon Him for comfort. Realizing that He is supporting us. Not seeking what God can do for us, but what He can do through us. Joy is in bearing fruit, even in times of adversity, suffering and trial.

Robert Ozment in his book *But God Can*, suggests six things we do well to remember while we are walking under the black shadow of tragedy and grief.

1. Do not be afraid to face trouble. It is impossible to solve any problem if we are afraid. Jesus was constantly telling people not to be afraid.

2. Remember that God has created a universe in which He permits trouble. That is not to say that God is the instigator of the trouble we know, but it is conceivable that God would sometimes send us trouble in order for us to achieve a higher good. Jesus lived the will of God to perfection, yet, at the end of His life, He found a cruel cross. Righteous living does not assure a life without trouble.

3. Remember that God is with us in our troubles. More than we realize it, God is in the midst of the struggle, commanding His forces.

4. We should be grateful to know that God will supply the strength we need to face life cheerfully during periods of trouble. If there is no way around it, God

provides a way through it. If one door is closed, God opens another for us. God's power is available to us.

5. Remember that God can use our troubles for our own good as well as for the good of others. Romans 8:28.

6. We should always remember that we are never alone. Matthew 28:20. God is always with us. He is able to help us.

When tragedy strikes us or our loved ones, we tend to blame God. We reason that He had the power to prevent it. Then we begin to feel that He should have prevented it. Without realizing it, we who are mortal, position ourselves in the seat of judgment and condemn God who is immortal and above all. In doing that, we envelop ourselves in a cloud of bitterness and anger. We become antagonistic toward the Lord's purposes for our lives. We remove ourselves from the game and become benched, while blaming God for our misfortune.

David Seamands discusses three aspects of the will of God in his book, *Putting Away Childish Things*: the intentional and perfect will of God, the circumstantial and permissive will of God, and the ultimate will and purpose of God. He states, "It is time we get rid of unbiblical notions which lead us to believe that everything which happens in this world today is the will of God. The intentional will of God is God's perfect will for us and for the world. However, the perfect will of God can be temporarily defeated by the will of man and the forces of evil. If this were not true, humans would have no real freedom to choose. There are a thousand and one tragedies which are the furthest from God's intentions for those situations. You may call these things evil, the fruit of human sin, accidents or the inevitable consequences of personal and social sin, but do not call them the intended and planned will of God. Man's free will creates circumstances that cut across God's plans and the fallen cosmos is effected by imperfection that goes through all of nature with its disasters."

My mother attempted on numerous occasions to witness to a neighbor of hers about the joy she was experiencing in living for Jesus, but each time her words were abruptly cut off. With beady eyes and rude sternness, her neighbor would rasp, "I don't want to hear about your God. We can talk about other things, but not that."

One day my mother, using all the tact she could muster, became more insistent in speaking about her faith. Again she was rudely stopped. However, she learned the reason for her neighbor's coldness. Her neighbor put forth a challenge, "If you can tell me why God took my husband twenty years ago when he was a clean living man who didn't drink or smoke, and why He left bums live that deserved to die, then I'll listen to what you have to say. I've asked this question to every minister I ran into since my husband died and not one of them could give me an answer."

After some reflection, my mother replied, "No one but God can answer that question. We must recognize that God is God. He loves us deeply and desires to heal our hurts. But He will not penetrate hearts we have chosen to close."

When my own father died, his death was not anticipated. It saddened my family greatly. But I will never forget his funeral service. It was a time of celebration. Singing and rejoicing! Did we wonder "why"? Yes. Did we receive an answer? No. Did we cry? Yes. Tears of sorrow and tears of joy. Through faith we believed that God cared, that He loved and that He knew. That was sufficient. And we were free to ask, "Now that this has happened, what is your will for us, God?"

The experience of permanent disability as the result of a sudden accident or a relentless disease often inflicts a degree of suffering similar to that of bereavement over the death of a loved one. Such suffering can become even more intense when accompanied by lasting physical pain.

Tim Hansel, founder of Summit Expedition, a wilderness survival school in the Sierras, had his life dramatically changed when his crampons balled up with snow and caused him to fall while attempting to navigate across an ice bridge. His body that moments before exhibited robust physical strength became racked with outrageous pain. His adventuresome spirit gave way to extreme disorientation and depression. In his book *You Gotta Keep Dancin'*, he vividly related the details of his struggle to deal with severe lifelong pain.

"Slowly my rage to live emerged from the depression, frustration and anger. I began to realize that it wasn't my imposed limitations that held me back as much as my perception of those limitations. It wasn't the pain that was thwarting me as much as it was my attitude toward the pain. I realized that though the difficulties were undeniably real, and would remain so for the rest of my life, I had the opportunity to choose a new freedom and joy if I wanted to. There is no such thing as a problem that doesn't have a gift in it. It's a matter of beginning to find some of those gifts and opening them."

Four years after his accident, he wrote about the benefits he experienced from his pain in his personal journal.

"This pain has forced some kind of awakening in me. It has established not only a new durability of spirit and a new endurance of heart, but also a wild and tenacious vividness of life. It is as though I've been forewarned- therefore, blessed - by the ensuing and insistent pain. Slowly I'm even learning to trust the pain like a friend, to learn from it like a mentor, embrace it like a brother and laugh at it."

Our God is faithful. As we tap into His vast resources we will experience the priceless promise of His word that He will "bestow ... the oil of gladness instead of mourning, and a garment of praise instead of a spirit of despair." Isaiah 61:3, NIV.

Frank H Leaman

*THAT HE WOULD
GRANT YOU,
ACCORDING TO THE
RICHES OF HIS GLORY,
TO BE STRENGTHENED
WITH MIGHT
BY HIS SPIRIT
IN THE INNER MAN.
EPHESIANS 3:16.*

Frank H Leaman

Victim of Abuse

Abuse can be emotional, physical, or psychological. It holds the power to exact feelings of extreme shame and worthlessness. Many struggle through life because they were dealt abuse in their personal histories that denied them healthy views of self-love. Deep within their spirits are gaping wounds that defy healing. Their hurts weigh them down and prevent them from experiencing wholeness of spirit, soul and body. Such wounds often cause personal crises and problems in relating to others. They find themselves searching for wholeness amid the dysfunction they experience in relationships with significant others.

Sexual abuse contaminates core beliefs about self that are carried within from childhood. These core beliefs shame, blame and condemn the inner being, often keeping the concept of the unconditional love of God from becoming an experiential reality. Victims may be able to acknowledge God's love with the head, but are far from knowing it as a heartfelt adventure of acceptance.

Adults who have been sexually abused in the past are often benched by an inner condemnation that confines them to the sidelines. Frozen in fear, they simply cannot perform in the present without first confronting the realities that crushed them in the past. This is both painful and threatening. Recovery necessitates the uncovering of experiences they have tried to forget. They need to be willing to work at changing the very core beliefs that have motivated decisions and relationships for many years. Despite the dysfunctionality of one's motivations, there is a certain degree of comfort with them that must be challenged and changed. The tough and heart-rending choice is that of risking the chance to go beyond negative core beliefs or stay on the bench.

One of my brothers is a minister. In studying for his Doctorate in Theology, he took courses to prepare himself to become proficient in counseling. A young woman who had been sexually abused as a child was among those who sought his help. She slithered into a chair in his office with tears streaming down her face. She came with a deluge of marital problems and a flood of physical symptoms of stress from stomach pain to headaches. People knew her as a fine Christian woman. It was very difficult for her to say no when asked to help with something, so she was recognized as a good worker in the church. Quite a pay-off for dysfunction. A way to feel holy when her past left her far less than whole.

Through counseling, it became evident that her unwillingness to say no as an adult had grown from an internalized shame and fear of rejection carried over from times past when as a seven to nine year old she could not say no to her grandfather's fondling. And at the age of sixteen, she didn't say no to a man who raped her. Hurting, hating and crying inside, she took on the guilt that the perpetrators should have felt. Her grandfather stripped her of an innocence that began an unconscious spiral of self-condemnation and shame that culminated in negative core beliefs.

> I am bad.
> I am dirty.
> I am unwanted.
> I am unloved.
> I deserve disapproval, condemnation and punishment.
> I can't be trusted.
> My opinions don't count.

Paradoxically, the core beliefs that kept her from trusting herself contributed to her need to trust Christ. Fortunately her faith, more often than not, kept her within the confines of expected Christian character, but her dependence on Christ was not a healthy acceptance of freeing love that could convince her of her worth before herself, God and others.

My brother, as her pastor and counselor, showed her how her negative core beliefs stemmed from the sexual abuse she had experienced. To prevent her negative core beliefs from staying with her and potentially ruining future relationships, he advised her to seek help from a Christian therapist who specialized in assisting persons with overcoming shame.

Making a choice to seek professional therapy is much more preferable than surrendering to the common arguments frequently given.

> It's really not that big an issue.
> I've forgotten all that.

I don't want to hurt anybody with what happened.
It's water over the dam.
I'm only interested in working on my marriage problems.

Healing comes as persons suffering from abuse realize that much of how they see themselves and relate to others is contingent upon the negative core beliefs they began telling themselves in years past. To escape the tenacious pull toward the bench, it is necessary for those suffering from the horrors of abuse to go beyond the comfort zone of their dysfunction and allow God to touch them with wholeness.

Broken lives mend.
Self-love can be discovered.
Joy and peace can be found.

Joe, an acquaintance of mine, lost a friend to a tragic death. The young man in his early twenties set himself on fire. The victim of this tragedy had been raised in a harshly disciplined home and an ultraconservative fundamental church. Emotionally, he would have been diagnosed as a schizophrenic. Gifted in art, he drew many cartoons. Although people had difficulty understanding what his cartoons meant, his art was a way of expressing himself.

At home he was constantly put down. At his church he was told that he was demon possessed. Eventually things went so badly for him at home that he moved out. But sometime later, a man in the apartment next door shot himself. He became afraid to stay where he was and moved back home.

More misunderstanding.
More harsh criticism.
More denial of love.
More unbearable misery.

For years he heard voices speaking to him. Evil voices. His psychotic disorder was characterized by a twisted view of the real world and by abnormal ways of thinking, feeling and behaving. He lived in emotional pain. Then one day, in a final act of extreme desperation he ended his life in flames.

> No one really listened to him.
> No one sought to share his aloneness.
> No one came to comfort him.
> No one chose to love him.

The closest friend he had was my friend Joe, who was many miles away. So he was left feeling alone. No medication. No psychiatric counseling. Although he occasionally exchanged letters with Joe, the distance limited what my friend was able to do for him. And distance prevented Joe from sensing the degree of hopelessness he was feeling.

After his friend's death, Joe showed me several of the cartoons his friend had mailed to him. Cries for help were clearly evident in the art. One of the cartoons showed an adult holding a child's hand. A pile of apples on a counter. A sign, "Apples, five cents," frame two. The child asks for an apple. The reply is negative and a pulling of the child's small arm. Frame three. A repeat of frame two. Frame four. A repeat of frame three. Frame five. A repeat of frame four except that the boy is pulled further away from the apples. Frame six. A repeat of frame five with the child saying, "Why in the hell not?" Frame seven. Permission to have an apple is granted. Frame eight. The child is close to the pile of apples and hearts are drawn around in the air.

But for Joe's friend, the real message was, "You aren't worth a five cent apple." In reality, he was never given permission to have what he desired. His dreams. The things that really mattered to him. So he traded agony for flames. Life for Death.

Mankind has proven his ability to slay his fellows in diverse manners. Outright acts of violence on one hand and not caring enough to extend love on the other. How many have died because we failed to put action into our love? Real love is a precious gift.

> A gift of time to listen.
> A gift to hold and embrace.
> A gift to seek to understand.
> A gift to forgive and not condemn.

Alas, too often the suffering are kicked aside. Left to lie in their blood. Where are the Good Samaritans?

"Look unto the fields," Jesus said. They are white. Grain that should have already been harvested is falling to the ground wasted.

"Go ye," Jesus said. Which being interpreted is, "Get off your benches."

212

FOR MY THOUGHTS
ARE NOT YOUR THOUGHTS,
NOR ARE YOUR WAYS
MY WAYS
SAYS THE LORD.
FOR AS THE HEAVENS
ARE HIGHER THAN
THE EARTH,
SO ARE MY WAYS HIGHER
THAN YOUR WAYS,
AND MY THOUGHTS
THAN YOUR THOUGHTS.
ISAIAH 55:8,9.

Frank H Leaman

Missing God's Best

The players in the game are those persons who take to heart the invitation Jesus gave to become active participants in His Kingdom. He instructed everyone to seek the Kingdom first above everything else, because there is no greater calling in life than doing the will of our Creator. The worst thing that can ever happen to us is to miss the best that our Heavenly Father has designed for us. He wants to see us become winners. Sitting on the bench while others are active in the game is depressive and unproductive. But we all sit there at times. Some of us briefly. Some of us for most of our lives. God never directs us to sit there. He longs for us to be involved in utilizing our abilities and talents to minister to others.

Our delight, as David put it in his first Psalm, is in keeping the law of the Lord and meditating upon it always. Our joy is found in doing the will of our Creator, walking in the likeness of Jesus, our Savior, and living lives that exemplify His love and compassion. The prophet Isaiah felt the joy of God's presence at work in his life and wrote with exuberant joy:

> "I will greatly rejoice in the Lord,
> My soul shall be joyful in my God;
> For He has clothed me with the robe of righteousness,
> As a bridegroom decks himself with ornaments,
> As a bride adorns herself with her jewels."

Playing the game God's way is the source of real joy. A joy that is everlasting in scope and maximized in its intensity. A joy that springs forth within us like a fountain even in the midst of unpleasant and painful circumstances because it continually directs our focus to that which is ours for eternity.

When our world is turned upside down by difficulties and tragedies that come like a flood and sweep us off course, there is still hope for us. Even when we have torn gaping holes in our lives by a series of wrong choices, there is still hope for us. Nothing has the power to destroy us. The way back, however, doesn't lie in our self-sufficiency: it comes to us as we recognize our dependence on God's sovereign ability to change us within the plight of our circumstances.

We remain His beloved children. He brings His presence to us as we open our lives to Him. He cares about our troubles far more than we can imagine. While the adversity we experience makes little sense to us, and the stab wounds of pain and loss really hurt, we have the privilege and blessing of choosing God's grace and opening our hearts to all that He would teach us. Our God is light. He knows the way out of our darkness. He is eager to bring to us the balm of His healing love and make roadways in our wildernesses and rivers in our deserts to lead us from our benches into the roles He has planned for us to play in our lives.

Healing comes to us as we submit our adverse circumstances to the Spirit of God and seek God's guidance in and through them. We often want the circumstances changed, while God wants us to learn truths of His mercy, grace, love, guidance and sustaining power. By seeking release from the grip of our circumstances and entering the doors God opens for us, we expose ourselves to the working of His grace in us. God's grace is the seal of His intimacy in our lives. As we offer our situations to God, His grace overflows into all areas of our lives and fills us with hope and assurance. We can take great encouragement in the truth that God's ultimate plan for our lives - salvation from sin and eternal life in His presence - can never be frustrated by the nature or magnitude of the circumstances we experience. Our troubles, painful as they frequently are, can actually become a means to stimulate our spiritual vitality. Our circumstances do not need to control us. The choice is ours to make.

In our pain, however, we are often inclined to reject God's efforts to heal us in the midst of our troublesome circumstances. The Prophet Jeremiah likened God's people to marred vessels that resist His efforts to restore. Imperfections in the objects being formed are not the fault of the Potter. The clay is faulty. It is stubborn and unyielding in the Potter's hands. Unlike earthly clay that is incapable of contaminating itself, we are living clay to whom God has given the authority of choice. It is our stubborn will, our pride, our doubts and our fears that limit the Master's hand to fashion the masterpieces He desires.

In Psalm 5, the work of God among His people is also compared to a vineyard God planted on a very fruitful hill. He removed the stones from the soil, planted it with the choicest vine, placed a fence around it and built a tower in the center of it. He looked for a harvest of good grapes, but it brought forth wild grapes of little value. Whereupon He called His people into judgment and asked, "What could have been done more to my vineyard that I have not done in it? Wherefore, when I looked that it should bring forth grapes, brought it forth wild grapes?"

Jeremiah wrote about this strange vine also. "Yet I planted you a choice vine, wholly of pure seed. How then have you turned degenerate and become a wild vine?" Jeremiah 2:21. Our Creator is looking for value in us. For vessels He can fill to perform His work here on the earth. For lives that will be fruitful in service.

We are held responsible by our Maker to cultivate an environment in our lives that will allow proper growth.

Growing the seeds God plants requires a special kind of heart.

> A heart that recognizes its need. Revelation 3:17.
> A heart that seeks after God and His Kingdom. Matthew 6:33; Isaiah 55:6, 7.
> A heart that hears. Matthew 13:15; John 12:48.
> A heart that believes. John 3:16.
> A heart that is open to learning. Matthew 11:29.

Our wholeness is there for the asking. "Ask, and it will be given you; seek, and you will find; knock, and it will be opened to you. For everyone who asks receives, and he who seeks finds, and to him who knocks it will be opened." Matthew 7:7, 8.

Man's dilemma is couched in the words of the Prophet Isaiah, "Behold, the Lord's hand is not shortened that it cannot save, or His ear dull, that it cannot hear; But your iniquities have made a separation between you and your God, and your sins have hid His face from you, so that He does not hear." Isaiah 59:1, 2. "All have sinned and fall short of the glory of God." Romans 3:23. So the laws of God regarding sin apply to all of us.

> "The soul that sins shall die." Ezekiel 18:20.
> "For it is the blood that makes atonement for the soul." Leviticus 17:11.
> "Without the shedding of blood there is no forgiveness of sins." Hebrews 9:22.

Our sins are purged by accepting the gift of God, the blood shed by His beloved Son. Our sin is cleansed from us by believing in Jesus. Through His sacrificial death, the just for the unjust, we become recipients of all that the Good News proclaims.

> Sins forgiven. I John 1:9.
> Righteousness in God's sight. II Corinthians 5:21.
> Children of God. John 1:12.
> The Spirit of God within. I John 3:24.
> A new creation. II Corinthians 5:17
> Partakers of the Kingdom of Christ. Colossians 1:13.
> Eternal life. John 5:24.

We need to ask ourselves how much we are willing to allow God to touch our lives. How much do we want to be changed? He didn't send His Spirit just to fix us up a little. He desires to restore us fully so we can move onto the playing field. Our hearts need to be bent toward God to the extent that we covet His will above our own. Then, as we fellowship with Him, He is able to direct our steps and empower us and accomplish His desires in our lives.

> "What does the Lord your God require of you, but to fear the Lord your God, to walk in all His ways, to love Him, to serve the Lord your God with all your heart and with all your soul." Deuteronomy 10:12.

> "Sow for yourselves righteousness, reap the fruit of steadfast love; break up your fallow ground, for it is the time to seek the Lord, that He may come and rain salvation upon you." Hosea 10:12.

> "And the Lord will guide you continually, and satisfy your desire with good things, and make your bones strong; and you shall be like a watered garden, like a spring of water, whose waters fail not." Isaiah 58:11.

Our God has provided a way of hope for us. He cannot renege on His promises. This hope is secured for us as we open our hearts to Him and endure through obedience. Steadfast hope is making God's will our will and our delight. This hope is ours to enjoy as we move from our benches of pain, despair and complacency, and allow God to fashion us into vessels of His choosing so we are fit for the game.

Frank H Leaman

BLESSED ARE THOSE WHO ARE CALLED TO THE MARRIAGE SUPPER OF THE LAMB REVELATION 19:9

Frank H Leaman

Prepare for the Party

God has a party planned for all who are victorious in the game of living. It will be astoundingly wonderful. We are given a glimpse of the splendor of this party and the merriment of it in the story that Jesus told about the Prodigal Son. A boy who rebelled and went astray, spent and lost all he had in the pursuit of pleasure. Then he experienced the pain and loneliness of being benched. Finally, he came to his senses. He repented of his sinful ways and returned to his father. Rather than condemn and punish his son, the father held a great celebration party for him. There was feasting and music and dancing.

The young man came to his father by choice. Had he not come to his senses and made that choice, he would have missed the party.

Everyone is invited to come to the party, even society's outcasts. Jesus likened the invitation to a certain king who prepared a marriage feast for his son. The king dispatched his servants to invite those on his guest list, but many made light of the invitation, made excuses and went their way. Then the king commanded his servants to invite everyone they could find, even the poor and undeserving, and encourage them to come to his party. Many joyfully responded to the invitation.

God's invitation is very clear. John, the Revelator, wrote, "The Spirit and the Bride say, 'Come.' And let him who hears say, 'Come.' And let him that is thirsty come, let him who desires take the water of life without price." Revelation 22:17. The invitation to the party is an invitation to enter the Kingdom of God and enjoy its rapturous glory and splendor for eternity.

One day Jesus told a great multitude that the kingdom of heaven is like a man that sowed good seed in his field. But his enemy came in the darkness of night and scattered bad seeds among the wheat so that wheat and weeds appeared together. Jesus likened the good seed to the children of God and the weeds to the children of the devil. At harvest time, the weeds were gathered together and cast into a fire; but the righteous, Jesus said, would shine forth as the sun in the kingdom of their Father. He said, "Rejoice in that day, and leap for joy, for behold, your reward is great in heaven." Luke 6:23.

From the time of man's creation God desired to be with His people. He visited Adam and Eve in the cool of the evening in the beautiful garden He planted for them to enjoy. He commanded the children of Israel to build a tabernacle where He could meet and speak with Aaron, the priest, and dwell among His people and be their God. The book of Exodus concludes with the glory cloud of the Lord covering the tent of the congregation of Israel and the glory of the Lord filling the tabernacle.

And yet in our future, we are told that the Lord will create a new heaven and a new earth and will reign in Jerusalem and joy in His people. Then the holy city, the new Jerusalem, the city foursquare, measuring 1,321 miles on each side and 1,321 miles high, with its walls radiating jasper light and its foundations sparkling with red, yellow, orange, purple, blue, green and violet will descend to the new earth out of heaven and the King of Kings and Lord of Lords, the Creator who sustains the universe will establish His tabernacle with men forever and ever.

The Apostle John wrote about a vision he saw:

> "Then I saw a new heaven and a new earth; for the first heaven and the first earth had passed away, and the sea was no more. And I saw the holy city, new Jerusalem, coming down out of heaven from God, prepared as a bride adorned for her husband; and I heard a great voice from the throne saying, 'Behold, the dwelling of God is with men. He will dwell with them, and they shall be His people, and God himself will be with them.' And the city has no need of sun or moon to shine upon it, for the glory of God is its light, and its lamp is the Lamb. By its light shall the nations walk; and the kings of the earth shall bring their glory into it, and its gates shall never be shut by day - and there shall be no night there." Revelation 21:1-3; 23-25.

A glory supernal! Two billion three hundred million cubic miles of space within the tabernacle of God. His glorious throne room. The river of life lined with trees bearing perpetual fruits. The mansions of the saints. All lighted by the brilliance of the glory of God.

Our God will triumph and reign supreme among His people. His hearts desire and our hearts desire will at last be satisfied. No tears. No sickness. No pain. No hunger. No thirst. No aging. No death. Nothing that defiles. Robes of glistening white. Golden crowns. Harps playing. Angels singing. Palms waving. We will join in anthems of exuberant thanksgiving and praise. We will dance and play and reign with Him. Forever enraptured in His goodness. Forever enveloped in the inexhaustible riches of His love. This is the reward for those who leave the bench and participate in the game.

References

NOT BEING GENUINE

Jacobson, Marion. *Saints And Snobs*, Wheaton, Illinois, Tyndale House Publishers, 1972.

Miller, Keith. *A Second Touch*, Waco, Texas, Word Books, 1967.

FEAR

Patterson, Ben. *Waiting: Finding Hope When God Seems Silent*, Downers Grove, Illinois, Intervarsity Press, 1989.

Muller, George. *The Autobiography of George Muller*, Springdale, Pennsylvania, Whitaker House, 1984.

Maxwell, L.E. *Born Crucified*, Chicago, Illinois, Moody Press, 1945.

SELF-RIGHTEOUSNESS AND HYPOCRISY

Maxwell, L.E. *Born Crucified*, Chicago, Illinois, Moody Press, 1945.

Jacobson, Marion. *Saints And Snobs*, Wheaton, Illinois, Tyndale House Publishers, 1972.

LOW SELF-ESTEEM

Seamands, David A. *Healing for Damaged Emotions*, SP Publications, Inc., 1981.

Davis, Ron Lee. *Healing Life's Hurts*, Dallas, Texas, Word Publishing, 1986.

McGee, Robert. *The Search for Significance*, Pasadena, Texas, The Lockman Foundation, 1985.

COMPLACENCY

Patterson, Ben. *Waiting: Finding Hope When God Seems Silent*, Downers Grove, Illinois, Intervarsity Press, 1989.

Demarest, Gary W. *The Heart of the Faith*, Waco, Texas, Word Books, 1987.

GUILT

Dobson, James. *Emotions: Can You Trust Them?* Ventura, California, Regal Books, 1980.

ENVY AND JEALOUSY

Buscaglia, Leo. *Loving Each Other*, Thorofare, New Jersey, SLACK Incorporated, 1984.

DOUBTING GOD

Eareckson, Joni with Musser, Joe. *Joni*, Grand Rapids, Michigan, Zondervan Publishing House, 1976.

DISOBEYING GOD'S DIRECTIVES

Finney, Charles G. *Prevailing Prayer*, Grand Rapids, Michigan, Kregel Publications, 1965.

HURT

Bosch, Henry G. *Rainbows for God's Children in the Storm*, Grand Rapids, Michigan, Radio Bible Class, 1981.

FAILURE TO FORGIVE

Smedes, Lewis B. *Forgive and Forget: Healing the Hurts We Don't Deserve*, San Francisco, California, Harper and Row Publishers, 1984.

GREED

Augsburger, Myron S. *Called To Maturity*, Scottdale, Pennsylvania, Mennonite Publishing House, 1960.

DISCOURAGEMENT AND DEPRESSION

Davis, Ron Lee. *Healing Life's Hurts*, Dallas, Texas, Word Publishing, 1986.

Adams, Nate. *Waking Up Down*, Decision Magazine, February, 1998.

MISPLACED TRUST
Maxwell, L.E. *Born Crucified*, Chicago, Illinois, Moody Press, 1945.

OVERCONFIDENCE
Anderson, Neil. *Victory Over the Darkness*, Ventura, California, Regal Books, 1990.

BEREAVEMENT AND PERSONAL TRAGEDY
Bolton, Leonard. *China Call*, Springfield, Missouri, Gospel Publishing House, 1984.

Ozment, Robert. *But God Can*, Westwood, New Jersey, Fleming H. Revell Company, 1962.

Seamands, David. *Putting Away Childish Things: Reaching For Spiritual and Maturity in Christ,* Wheaton, Illinois, SP Publications, 1982.

Hansel, Tim. *You Gotta Keep Dancin'*, Elgin, Illinois, David C. Cook Publishing Co., 1985.

About the Author

Born in Africa to missionary parents, Frank's early life was a kaleidoscope of cultural diversity and experiences shaped by a strong religious heritage. Upon the family's return to the States to live on a small farm in central Pennsylvania, Frank's father pastored a Mennonite congregation where Frank began a life commitment to serving God. He became active in lay ministry while he pursued a Bachelor of Arts Degree in chemistry and Bible Studies at Eastern Mennonite College in Harrisonburg, Virginia. Frank followed a career in industry as a research chemist, engineering manager and entrepreneur; but always sensing the call to ministry, Frank enrolled in graduate courses in Theology at Bethany Seminary, Richland, Indiana. He became a minister and is currently serving as the pastor of West Shore Church of the Brethren in Enola, Pennsylvania.

Frank writes and presents the radio program *Moments With God* that airs weekly in the central Pennsylvania area. He is also the founder and president of Jehovah-Jireh Ministries, Ltd., a ministry established to provide assistance to national pastors and evangelists in foreign countries.

After being widowed for four years, Frank recently remarried and lives with his wife Sheryl in Dallastown, Pennsylvania. He has four children, three stepchildren, and six grandchildren.

Printed in the United States
1017000003B

9 781403 348913